T0309380

ATING
ANE

YARD

# RUM – RHUM – RON

**COVER PHOTO:**

*Jamaica around 1880. (Bridgeman Images)*

For centuries, people were deported from Africa to the Caribbean and enslaved for the gruelling work of sugar production. We dedicate this book to them.

# RUM – RHUM – RON

PASCAL KÄHLIN
WITH SINA BÜHLER

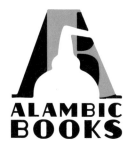

ALAMBIC
BOOKS

# CONTENTS

*Pressing sugarcane in Mexico (Photo: Carlos R. Cervantes)*

*"Bagasse" – pressed sugarcane, Granada*

*The sugarcane is delivered, Marie-Galante*

# SUGAR

In 325 BC, a general from the army of Alexander the Great came across a plant that produced "honey, without the help of bees", as he described in wonder. It was sugarcane. The plant had presumably come from New Guinea, where the giant grass had been cultivated for a long time. In the 6th century, it came as far as Europe: the Arabic-Moorish expansion brought it to the Iberian peninsula – it is said that "sugar followed the Quran".

Back then, sugar was a new and totally different condiment. It was not only used to sweeten baked goods, but also to season soups and meat. And it was expensive: in 1319 it cost "two shilling a pound" in England – today that would be the equivalent of 120 Euros per kilogram.

However, the Mediterranean climate only had a limited suitability for cultivation – the African north coast was too hot and dry; the winter in Europe was too frosty. The harvest was rather scarce for the work that had to be put into cultivation on Crete, Sicily, and Cyprus.

The plant therefore travelled on. In 1425 Henry the Navigator, the patron of Portuguese exploratory expeditions, gave his crew Sicilian sugar plants to take with them and plant on Madeira, which had recently seen its first inhabitants. The harvest there was soon so enormous that the Spaniards also got a taste for it and tried to do the same on Gomera, one of the Canary Islands. At the time it was refined exclusively on the mainland; after all, as much profit as possible was to flow into the cities' pockets. To Venice, for example, which together with Antwerp and Bruges already had a monopoly on the sugar trade in the 13th century. Or to Genoa, where the most well-known son of the city came into contact with it: the family of the first wife of Christopher Columbus had become rich with it. When he set off to the New World at the behest of Spain, he already had experience in the sugar trade between Madeira and Genoa.

Hence Columbus packed a few sprigs on the Canary Islands and took them with him on his second journey to the Caribbean. Columbus, the sugar expert, thought that Hispaniola – the island that the present-day Dominican Republic and Haiti lie on – would be ideal. And indeed, the cane did not take more than seven days to take root in the soil and to shoot upwards. The tropical plant thrived so magnificently that soon a real industry sprang up around it and in Hispaniola alone there were a hundred factories. However, it did not last long: as early as 1600 there were only eleven factories left. Instead of sweating on plantations, the Spanish adventurers preferred to go for the valuable metals of which they found an abundance on the American mainland. The trade monopoly, state interventions, and high customs duties in Spain also played their part in hindering the growth of the sugar industry.

Sugar was therefore to become a success story for another major seafaring nation. In the meantime, the Portuguese had planted sugar not only in Madeira, but also on the islands of Sao Tomé and Principe. Portugal thereby soon rose to be the largest producer in the world. When the new colony Brazil was added in 1500, the Portuguese needed barely twenty years to develop their sugar imperium to scarcely imaginable dimensions.

Brazil was now the richest colony in the world. This brought the Netherlands onto the map, by now the largest trading and banking power in Europe. For several years, the Dutch succeeded in bringing a couple of coastal areas in Bahia under control for a short period. In 1630 they conquered a little further to the north, the whole province surrounding present-day Recife. As the governor of Dutch Brazil had introduced religious freedom to the colony, soon many Dutch Jews settled there. The Dutch quickly brought production back on track and the export volume rose strongly owing to their trade ships.

However, the cooperation between the Calvinist Dutch and the local Portuguese plantation owners worked only partially. Some poor harvests, which were presumably due to the now depleted soil, prompted the Dutch to expand into the Caribbean in the middle of the 17<sup>th</sup> century. When the Dutch troops lost the Battle of Guararapes in 1654, many were driven away.

Sugar production brought a trade triangle: ships from Europe sailed with materials, weapons, metal, and glassware to Africa, where these goods were exchanged for slaves. The Europeans sailed on across the Atlantic, sold the slaves to the plantations and made their way back to Europe with products and raw materials, including sugar.

At the same time, a sugar replacement was being sought in Europe, a plant that would also grow in cooler regions. Although Olivier de Seres had discovered the sweet taste of a previously scarcely noticed beet – the sugar beet – back in 1590, it was almost another two centuries before sugar could be extracted from it. Andreas Sigismund Marggraf was the first to achieve this in 1747.

Today sugar is produced in 130 countries – of which 20 percent is from the beet that is primarily cultivated in the north. However, the majority is still sugarcane from the south. The largest producers are Brazil (almost 40 percent of worldwide exports), Thailand, and India. Something else that has not changed: trade still runs through Europe, with 50 percent of transit trade via Swiss companies.

# RUM

Just as sugar is said to have followed the Quran, rum followed sugar. It did not take long for the sugar industry in the Caribbean to form the basis for rum production, whose starting product must always be sugarcane.

Arrack (page 166), a spirit that has now almost been forgotten, played a decisive role in its development history. It is considered one of the oldest spirits in the world and enjoyed a high esteem. Marco Polo reports about it for the first time in his travel report *Il Milione* that was published at the beginning of the 14<sup>th</sup> century. It was then presumably Genoese merchants that brought it to Europe.

*Freshly distilled rum, Martinique*

They soon attempted to imitate the imported and enormously popular Asian arrack with local raw ingredients. This was achieved particularly well and productively with sugarcane, which had only been planted few years before on the new estates in Portugal. The earliest spirits in Europe that were distilled out of sugarcane – and were "rum" from a current point of view – were presumably created on the Canary Islands or Madeira. It is quite possible that the Portuguese took the rum production technology with them to Brazil, which had been accorded to them in 1494 (page 124). They called the drink by the name it still has today – "cachaça". There is also the theory, however, that the honour is due to the Dutch who had settled near present-day Recife in 1629. In any case, the earliest verified rum production on a larger scale developed around 1640 in Dutch Brazil, presumably out of sugarcane juice, although the drink only became great in Barbados (page 29). It was produced out of molasses there, a thick, sticky, black-brown syrup that remains as residue during sugar production. It is thinned with water, enriched with yeast and then fermented. The plantation owners had noticed that they could earn even more with the residue of the already extremely profitable sugar business by making the cheapest alcohol for the poorest and slaves out of it. Rum had definitively arrived in the world.

In the early stages of rum production, of course there was no talk of fine spirits being stored in casks. Rum was only stored if it could not be flogged off immediately. For a long time, it was considered a drink for slaves, pirates, and poor people. Its old names such as "Rumbullion" (turmoil, commotion) or "Kill Devil" (because it was so strong) show its value at the time. Even among the British Royal Navy, where it replaced the previously served beer upon pressure from the West Indian plantation owners, the drink was initially reserved for the simple sailors. The higher ranks continued to drink Spanish brandy. The British Navy helped greatly to spread this spirit with their immense consumption. Every day each sailor received half a pint (approx. 2.84 dl). From 1740 onwards, this good quarter of a litre was divided into two rations, prompted by Admiral Vernon, diluted with water and enriched with lemon juice. He thereby invented grog (page 194), one of the oldest cocktails in the world alongside punch and julep.

15

There are countless technical possibilities for distillation that can result in different styles of rum. The greatest role is played by the distillation device, of which there are basically two different types. The original form is the alembic, which has existed since the Middle Ages. This is discontinuous distilling apparatus that is usually called "pot still" today. The mash is filled into it, heated and distilled. When the distilling process has ended the pot must be emptied, then refilled and reheated. This elaborate technique results in distillates rich in content.

The second type is the continuous column apparatus named the "Coffey still" after Aeneas Coffey, or nowadays often "column still". There are countless forms and derivations of it. The basic principle is that the mash is fed into the top and steam into the bottom of a big column that has various so-called bubble trays. Alcohol of varying volume strengths condenses on the individual trays. It is extracted from where the required strength is. This system allows distilling without interruption, saving personnel and costs. With a column, alcohol is distilled at a high volume; it is cleaner and usually less aromatic.

The producers leave the finished white rum as a 100 % ("overproof") or they dilute it with water to drinking strength. Sometimes it is stored for years in chrome steel tanks and filtered through activated carbon.

For a dark, mature rum to develop, the white rum is stored in casks. Storage can be in cool cellars or in hot metal sheds, in the Caribbean or in Europe, in small or large casks (such as disused American bourbon casks) but there are no limits to experimentation in this regard. It is also possible for port, sherry, cognac, wine, or newly made casks to be used. The "blender" chooses the best combinations from the various casks and creates a dark, mature rum.

If a particularly good cask is filled separately into bottles, one speaks of a "single cask" filling. Today there are a relatively high number of independent fillers who buy individual casks and put the rum on the market with their own label. However, for storage there is increasing use of the more economical Solera system, which comes from sherry production. This involves building a cask pyramid and drawing part of the contents from the bottom row for sale. Then it is refilled with younger rum from the top row downwards. This means that if it

*A disused column still, Martinique*

*A pot still in Jamaica (Photo: Worthy Park)*

says "Solera 23" on a bottle, the smallest contained proportion is at least twenty-three years old, but the majority is significantly younger.

Traditionally, rather light-body rums are prevalent on the Spanish-speaking islands of the Caribbean. Especially in Cuba, where this style was invented by Facundo Bacardí. The rum is mild and fruity, due in part to an active carbon filtration that it runs through after distillation. Continuous column stills are primarily used here. Barbados, the second largest sugar island after Cuba, stands on the other hand for the English medium-body style. Rum from pot stills and column stills are usually mixed for this purpose.

The heaviest rums in the world are still produced in Jamaica, the third largest sugar island, and Guyana. There used to be over 150 sugarcane plantations here and just as many distilleries. They are often pure pot-still distillates that result in a heavy-body rum, which is of particular significance especially for the British navy style.

The Spanish-speaking countries in Latin America leave the rum somewhat heavier and mostly very sweet. They prefer the Solera system for storage. They have the shortest tradition for rum production and have therefore forged a modern style that has become very successful in recent years. A considerable amount of sugar is often added to the ready-distilled rum, which makes it rounded and more easily drinkable. However, added sugar always obscures some of the true flavour.

On the French-speaking islands, as well as in Brazil and a small number of other distilleries, rum is not distilled from molasses but directly from sugarcane juice. This is then called rhum agricole – or cachaça in Brazil. The taste of the white rhum agricole is usually somewhat sharper and more vegetal than the sweeter molasses rum. When matured it provides wonderful, very characteristic drinks. White rum is perfect for a "Ti' Punch" (page 190).

However, distillation today is increasingly neither from molasses nor sugarcane juice, but from sugar syrup. As a rule, this is nothing other than boiled up sugarcane juice. It makes it last and so the distillery is no longer bound to seasons, as fresh sugarcane juice ferments very quickly and must be processed within a short time frame. If syrup is referred to as sugarcane juice it is a palliation, as it is rather light molasses or the so-called "first molasses".

It is not very easy to classify the various rum styles. Older books mostly speak of "light-body", "medium-body", and "heavy-body", other sources of the Spanish, French, or British style. For the country-specific classification, it can be said in a very simplified manner that the Spanish rum is orientated towards brandy (rather light, sweetish, linear aroma), French rum towards cognac (rather heavy, complex aroma) and the British rum towards whisky (heavy, strong, accented by the cask). As everywhere, of course for each form of classification there are exceptions – or rum that cannot really be allocated to any classification.

For clarification: alcohol becomes "cleaner" through repeated distillation and gains a texture that feels lighter. Vodka, for example, is a very clean alcohol. Lighter sorts of rum are usually made in continuously working column stills – the cleaner the alcohol, the less aromatic the rum is.

Heavy types of rum are typically made in discontinuous pot stills. They still contain certain proportions of fusel oils, aromas, ethanol, and other alcohols and some have an almost oily texture. Scottish single-malt whisky is distilled exclusively with pot-still apparatus. The medium-heavy rums are often mixes of pot-still and column-still distillates.

I have tried to order the rums listed by indicating the heaviness, the sweetness, the starting material, and the type of distillation apparatus.

Richness and sweetness on a scale from 1 to 5:

🍾 = light; 🍾🍾🍾🍾🍾 = very rich

⬡ = not sweet; ⬡⬡⬡⬡⬡ = very sweet

Starting material:

♣ = molasses, 🎋 = sugarcane juice, 🌢 = sugarcane syrup

Type of distillation still:

⚗ = pot still, 🏭 = column still

**yo**: years in the barrel

CANADA

UNITED STATES

MEXICO

CUBA

THE BAHAMAS

Turks and Caicos
Islands (U.K.)

JAMAICA

HAITI

DOMINICAN
REPUBLIC

Puerto Rico
(U.S.)

ST. KITTS
& NEVIS

ANTIGUA AND BARBUDA

Guadeloupe (FR.)

DOMINICA

Martinique (FR.)

ST. LUCIA

BARBADOS

BELIZE

GUATEMALA

HONDURAS

EL SALVADOR

NICARAGUA

COSTA RICA

PANAMA

ST. VINCENT AND
THE GRENADINES

GRENADA

TRINIDAD AND
TOBAGO

VENEZUELA

GUYANA

SURI-
NAME

COLOMBIA

ECUADOR

Galapagos Islands
(ECUADOR)

BELIZE

HONDURAS

LA

ADOR

NICARAGUA

COSTA RICA

PANAMA

HAITI    DOMINICAN
         REPUBLIC

ST. KITTS
& NEVIS

Guadeloupe (FR.)

DOMINICA

Martinique (FR.)

ST. VINCENT AND
THE GRENADINES

ST. LUCIA

GRENADA

BARBADOS

TRINIDAD AND
TOBAGO

VENEZUELA

COLOMBIA

GUYANA

SURI-
NAME

Fr.
Guiana
(FR.)

s Islands
DOR)

ECUADOR

PERU

B R A Z I L

BOLIVIA

PARAGUAY

CHILE

URUGUAY

ARGENTINA

Falkland Islands
(U.K.)

23

FLORIDA
(U.S.)

Grand
Bahama

Abaco
Islands

New
Providence

Ele

Florida Keys

Andros

T H E

G
Ex

Isla de la
Juventud

C U B A

CAYMAN ISLANDS
(U.K.)

Lesser
Caymans

Grand
Cayman

JAMAICA

AMAS

*rooked*
*Island*

*Acklins*

*Mayaguana*

**TURKS
AND CAICOS
ISLANDS**
(U.K.)

*Caicos Islands*

*Inagua
Islands*

*Turks Islands*

*Tortuga*

**HAITI**

*Hispaniola*

*Gonâve Island*

*Île-à-Vache*

**DOMINICAN
REPUBLIC**

*Beata
Island*

*Saona
Island*

*Isla de
Mona*

*Vieques*

**PUERTO
RICO**
(U.S.)

HAITI **PORT-AU-
PRINCE**

**SANTO
DOMINGO**

S

DOMINICAN
REPUBLIC

PU
I

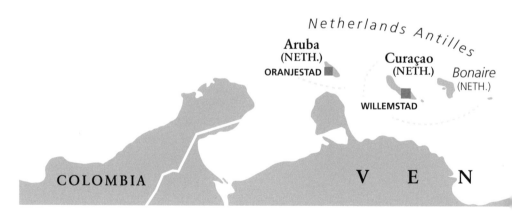

*Netherlands Antilles*

**Aruba**
(NETH.)
ORANJESTAD

**Curaçao**
(NETH.)

*Bonaire*
(NETH.)

WILLEMSTAD

COLOMBIA

V E N

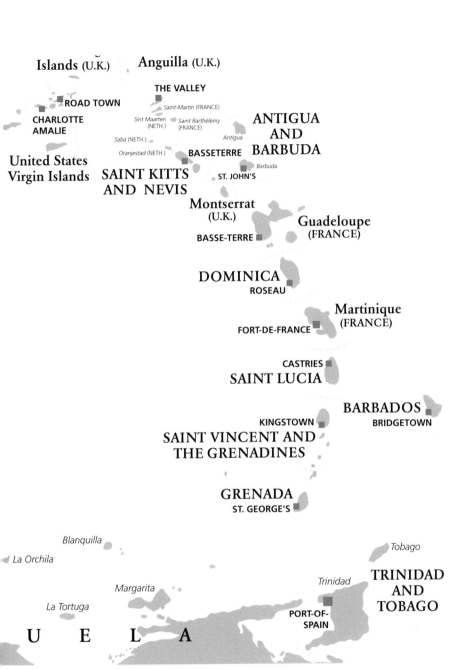

Islands (U.K.)  Anguilla (U.K.)

THE VALLEY
ROAD TOWN
Saint-Martin (FRANCE)
CHARLOTTE
AMALIE
Sint Maarten
(NETH.)
Saint Barthélemy
(FRANCE)
ANTIGUA
AND
BARBUDA
Saba (NETH.)
Antigua
United States
Virgin Islands
Oranjestad (NETH.)
BASSETERRE
SAINT KITTS
AND NEVIS
ST. JOHN'S
Barbuda

Montserrat
(U.K.)
Guadeloupe
(FRANCE)
BASSE-TERRE

DOMINICA
ROSEAU

Martinique
(FRANCE)
FORT-DE-FRANCE

CASTRIES
SAINT LUCIA

BARBADOS
BRIDGETOWN
KINGSTOWN
SAINT VINCENT AND
THE GRENADINES

GRENADA
ST. GEORGE'S

Blanquilla
Tobago
La Orchila
Trinidad
TRINIDAD
AND
TOBAGO
Margarita
La Tortuga
PORT-OF-
SPAIN
U E L A

*West Indies Rum Distillery, Barbados (Photo: Stefan Kerner)*

# BARBADOS

This flat coral island – one of the few in the Caribbean that is not of volcanic origin – has given itself the title of the birthplace of rum. The Portuguese came ashore on the unpopulated island in 1536 when they were on their way to Brazil. They called it "Los Barbudos" after the Bengal fig trees that were widespread there, whose gigantic aerial roots look like beards. In the past, the indigenous people, the Siboneys, had been driven away by the Arawak, who in turn had fled from the bellicose Caribs who left the island again later. After the Portuguese had also moved on, the Englishman Sir William Curteen appeared in 1627 with a handful of settlers to revitalize the island. First, they planted tobacco, based on the model of the English colony Virginia. However, this did not suit the competition – the North American colonies – at all. They put London under pressure, whereupon Barbados tobacco was set with massive taxes. The settlers switched to sugarcane out of necessity. They were to have so much success with this that Barbados was soon called "Little England". The few families that shared the sugar business in Barbados, the so-called "sugar barons", achieved enormous wealth within a short time. They soon diluted the residual molasses with water, fermented it and distilled it to rum. The alcohol, now called "Kill Devil", was drunk especially by slaves and the poor. The wealthy Englishmen then still drank brandy and Madeira. The only form in which these higher classes drank the raw slave drink was punch. The Swiss doctor Felix Christian Spöri wrote in 1661: "One takes a basin of water and sweetens it with sugar, then lemon juice, and finally the above-mentioned Kill Devil or brandy". The slaves and labourers were also given rum as medicine against "weakness and decline in mind or body", according to the author and contemporary witness Richard Ligon. The name rum could also have originated in Barbados. The Connecticut House of Assembly calls the spirits "whatsoever Barbados liquors, commonly called Rum, Kill Devil or the like" in a law for their confiscation in 1657. In the book *The Distiller of London*, published in 1639, one can find the recipe for "Barbados Water", a mix of various spices, alcohol, and sugar. With great imagination, one can view this spirit as a precursor to rum, although it is thought that at this time a spirit was already being distilled in Brazil (page 124) that was somewhat closer to rum. Today Barbados uses modern column stills and traditional pot stills to produce the classical English medium-body style that is very balanced and elegant.

## R. L. Seale & Co. Ltd.

This is one of the last rum enterprises that is exclusively in the hands of a Barbadian – namely the fourth generation. Distillation takes place at the Foursquare Distillery with column stills and pot stills – as is typical of Barbados. The distillery was founded in the 17th century and ownership was later passed to R. L. Seale & Co. It was completely renovated in 1996 to become one of the most modern distilleries in the Caribbean. Today the distillery is run by Sir David Seale and his son Richard. Richard Seale is also the master distiller and enjoys the greatest respect in the rum community. He is considered one of the leading heads of a movement that stands for producing rum authentically and without any additives or additional sugar.

### *Doorly's xo*

*The name of this rum goes back to the Doorly family. The merchants from Bridgetown bought various rums, blended them, and put their own label on the bottle. It was stored in whisky and then in Oloroso sherry casks. A balanced, sweetish medium-body rum with character.*

## Real McCoy 12 years
🍾🍾🍾 / 🧊🧊🧊 / 🥄 / ⚗️ & 🧴

*This rum has an exciting history in many ways. The name refers to Bill McCoy. In January 1920, just after the prohibition came into effect, he was one of the first to sail to the Caribbean with a ship called a "rum runner", filling it completely with alcohol and returning to New York with it, anchoring three nautical miles in front of the coast. There he was in international waters and was able to operate a kind of floating spirit business. Many emulated him – but most cut their alcohol with all kinds of things. McCoy was known for having a very good, uncut product, which is why the term "the real McCoy" established itself for especially good spirits. Almost a hundred years later, Baily Pryor started to produce a documentary film about Bill McCoy for American television. During his research on Barbados, his fascination for rum grew. He found a perfect partner in Richard Seale to produce a rum as it was supposed to have been during the prohibition era. The documentary film won five Emmy Awards, the rum many prizes. And today Bailey Pryor is more at home in the rum than in the film business. The twelve-year-old rum is beautifully balanced with a very pleasant sweetness. A perfect example of a very well-made, medium-body rum.*

## R. L. Seale's 10 yo
🍾🍾🍾 / 🧊🧊🧊🧊 / 🥄 / ⚗️ & 🧴

*This rum comes in a rather special bottle. It is supposed to evoke the leather bottles that sailors carried with them in the past. In the first instance, however, it is a very accomplished, balanced rum that shows what good "blending" means. The mix is decisive – and Richard Seale is a master of this. Column- and pot-still rum of varying ages, stored in ex-bourbon, Madeira, and cognac casks.*

# W. I. R. D.

The world-famous Malibu, amongst other things, is produced at the West Indies Rum Distillery. Even so, the W. I. R. D. is also capable of producing extremely sophisticated, heavy rums. The distillery called Black Rock Distillery in the vernacular has two columns of four, along with two old pot stills. These produce the heavy distillates full of character. In 1893 it was the first distillery in Barbados to procure a column still. W. I. R. D. was acquired by the French cognac producer Maison Ferrand in spring 2017, which runs the rum line Plantation alongside its cognac business. With the acquisition, W. I. R. D.'s third of the National Rums of Jamaica (NRJ) also went to Maison Ferrand (page 50).

## Cockspur V. S. O. R.

This rum was launched in 1984 and still bears the same name. The abbreviation stands for "Very Special Old Reserve" and is a wholly classical Barbados rum. That means it is a blend of molasses rum from the column and pot stills. The majority lay in the former bourbon casks for more than twelve years.

## Barbados 2000 17 yo / Cave Guildive

This single-cask bottling of a heavy, pure pot-still rum is from the Swiss "bottler" Cave Guildive. The last two years of its maturation took place in Zurich. The full spectrum of what a good pot still is capable of is shown here: the whole sweetness molasses can provide, coupled with an incredible vibrancy of fruit, tea, and nut aromas.

# Mount Gay Rum Distillery

It is said that Abel and William Gay bought the St. Lucy Estate, where a little still also stood, in the north of Barbados in the year 1663. This is un-verified. The first real evidence that rum was distilled on this plantation, on the other hand, is a certificate of sale from the year 1703. Even so, the rum distillery is still entitled to call itself the "oldest in the world" that has produced continuously. In the beginning, various producers distilled here, until at the beginning of the 18th century William Sandiford purchased several plantations and joined them together as the Mount Gilboa plan-tation. In 1747 he sold the estates and facilities to John Sober, whose friend and confidant Sir John Gay Alleyne took over the management of the plantation. After his death in 1801, it was allegedly renamed Mount Gay in his honour, as there was already a Mount Alleyne.

Whether it is coincidence that the first owners were also called Gay, or whether it was the changing marketing departments of the owners who like to rewrite history a little, remains an open matter.

At the beginning of the 20th century, Audrey Ward – who is said to have had more than ninety children – acquired the distillery. It is with him that it gained its great renown, which it enjoys up until today. His son, Darnley DaCosta Ward, continued to lead the company successfully until his death in 1989. The Ward family sold the company that same year and with it the brand rights to the Rémy-Cointreau corporation. And suddenly even James Bond was drinking Mount Gay rum.

In 2014 there was some confusion about Mount Gay: the company was in financial difficulties and was supposed to have been closed, which was awkward for Rémy Cointreau. After all, the whole image of the brand rested on the legend of being the "oldest distillery in the world". Nevertheless, it did not belong to Rémy Cointreau: the corporation had only bought the company and the brand rights, but not the distillery itself. Rémy Cointreau announced that the Mount Gay Rum Refinery had been closed. A sister company produced rum for Mount Gay, but also for Mount Gilboa, which was new at the time. Rémy Cointreau went on to acquire these parts of the company and now controls production. In the meantime, more plantations in the area have been added.

### Mount Gay Eclipse

*The drawing card of the company. A cut of rum from both stills about two years old. Well-balanced medium-body rum. A good reference rum for this style.*

### Mount Gay XO

*The somewhat heavier and sweeter variety. A cut of seven- to ten-year-old rum largely from a pot still.*

### Mount Gilboa

*Frank Ward, a descendant of the aforementioned Aubrey Ward, tried to produce a rum somewhat richer in content to build on past times. When the rum refinery also went to Rémy Cointreau, however, the project soon came to an end again. The Mount Gilboa is, contrary to Mount Gay, a pure, triple-distilled rum from a pot still. It was stored for four years in used American oak casks.*

*West Indies Rum Distillery, Barbados (Photo: Stefan Kerner)*

*St. Nicholas Abbey, Barbados (Photo: Stefan Kerner)*

## St. Nicholas Abbey's

This beautiful manor house in the style of a Jacobin monastery was built between 1650 and 1660 at the foot of Cherry Tree Hill in St. Peter. Rum production started at the beginning of the 18th century. At this time, the property was sold to a certain Joseph Dottin, who in turn gave it to his daughter and her husband for their wedding. The recipient of the gift was none other than Sir John Gay Alleyne. Much later, he also ran the Mount Gay distillery that was named in his honour.

In the 20th century, the price collapse of sugar and the major competition presented difficulties to the plantation – it closed completely in 1947 and most of the equipment was sold. In 1983 the house was converted into a museum, which houses a perfect replica of the old steam mill.

In 2006, the Warren family purchased the St. Nicholas Abbey property and began to restore the old distillery. The company Arnold Holstein at Lake Constance manufactured apparatus that was a combination of a pot still and a column still and was planned specifically for the requirements of St. Nicholas Abbey. Consequently, after many years of cessation, rum is finally being produced again, if only in small quantities. Here, too, the busy "Master Distiller" of Foursquare, Richard Seale, was involved as an adviser.

The older rums with the name St. Nicholas Abbey also come from the stock of the Foursquare Distillery.

### St. Nicholas Abbey 5 yo Barbados Rum

🍾🍾 / 🧊🧊🧊 / 💧 / ⚗️ & 📦

*This is the first mature rum that was made completely in the new distillery. It was distilled out of sugarcane syrup, meaning boiled down sugarcane juice. After that it matures for five years in used bourbon casks. Due to the distilling apparatus, untypical of Barbados, it results in a rather light rum with a lovely bouquet.*

*Buccoo Bay, Tobago*

# TRINIDAD AND TOBAGO

The two islands of Trinidad and Tobago lie in front of Venezuela. They are the homeland of calypso, steel bands, and the famous Carnival. And of heavy rum. Like Barbados, they are also not of volcanic origin, but were once part of the South American mainland. Endemic species developed here accordingly, such as a glowing lizard. In 1498, Columbus came to the island and gave it the name Trinidad – trinity – inspired by its three mountain peaks. After twenty-five years in the ownership of the Spanish crown, the island was taken over by the British in 1797. In the following century, Trinidad rose to become the largest rum producer in the world, together with Guyana and Jamaica. Since 1889, the island has been governed together with Tobago. They were granted independence as a state within the Commonwealth in 1962.

In the rum world, Trinidad is known for the British Navy rum cuts. Rum from Trinidad, Jamaica, and Guyana has always formed its basis, as producers in these countries master the art of manufacturing extremely heavy-bodied rum like nobody else.

Unfortunately, many distilleries have disappeared over the years and today only one remains: the producer of the world-famous Angostura Bitter, which is manufactured on the basis of rum.

One of the most famous songs about rum also comes from Trinidad. The legendary calypso singer Lord Invader saw the American G.I.s mixing their Coca-Cola with Trinidad rum in 1942 and wrote the hit song "Rum and Coca-Cola" (page 46). However, the song only became famous later through the Andrew Sisters. Morey Amsterdam, who brought the song to the U.S. and to the Andrew Sisters, had not taken care of the copyright. Two plagiarism suits followed that only made the song more famous. The drink the song is about is actually nothing other than a Trinidad version of Cuba Libre.

## Angostura Ltd.

For the bars of this world, the most important thing this distillery offers us is the world-famous Angostura Bitter. The German doctor Dr. Johann Siegert developed it when he was twenty-four years old in 1820 in Venezuela. Siegert was then in the service of the independence fighter Simón Bolívar and used the bitter as a medicine against the feverish infections that the resistance fighters suffered from. His sons relocated the business to Trinidad in 1875. As Angostura Bitter is manufactured on a rum basis, Robert W. Siegert also started to distil his own rum in 1936.

Today Angostura Ltd. sells a whole range of rum of various quality standards and is a large producer of open rum ("bulk rum"), which is sold throughout the world.

### Angostura 1787

*The first sugarcane plantation is said to have been established in Trinidad in 1787 – the year in the name refers to this. It is the so-called "super premium rum" of the manufacturer and a blend of rum stored for at least fifteen years. A good product, made to have widespread appeal, yet it still maintains its own character.*

## Trinidad Distillers Ltd.

The distillery Trinidad Distillers is a division of Angostura – and the actual distillery. All types of rum are distilled here that are sold under the umbrella of Angostura. This column distillery is highly modern and capable of producing a wide range of rum styles. Apart from the rum for Angostura, a further 18 to 20 million litres of alcohol are distilled that go to producers and bottlers that do not distil themselves.

## Cadenhead's TMAH 24 yo
🍾🍾🍾🍾🍾 / 🎲🎲 / 🝆 / 🏭

*Cadenhead's buys individual casks or tanks from selected distilleries and finishes maturing them in Scotland. This one was stored in cold Scotland for 24 years.*
*It is evident straight away here what "heavy-body" means: extremely aromatic rum in cask strength.*

## Zaya Gran Reserva Rum 12 yo
🍾🍾🍾 / 🎲🎲🎲🎲 / 🝆 / 🏭

*This rum was originally distilled in Guatemala. However, when the major corporation Diageo took over marketing and sales of the now internationally famous Zacapa rum, it gave up the brand Zaya again for economic reasons. The production went to Trinidad Distillers and shows nicely how a modern distillery can produce various styles.*
*Zaya tastes as if it still came from Latin America: sweetish-mild.*

## Kraken Black Spiced Rum
🍾🍾 / 🎲🎲🎲🎲🎲 / 🝆 / 🏭

*This rum originally comes from Trinidad and is supposed to be matured for two years in casks. This is no longer very evident in this "spiced rum" with all its sugar and spices. Here it is primarily about the "packaging" and "corporate design" that a company from the U.S.A. thought up.*

# Caroni Distillers Ltd.

Caroni Distillers Ltd. was the rum division of the state agricultural enterprise Caroni Ltd., whose focus was on sugar. The company founded in 1937 by the British agricultural giant Tate & Lyle was taken over completely by the state of Trinidad in 1975. In state hands, the company always remained deficient due to poorly negotiated trade agreements and probably also political quarrels and had to close in 2003. 9,000 employees became unemployed and Trinidad has struggled since to find enough of its own molasses for rum production.

The rum produced at Caroni was an important component in British "navy rum". Extremely heavy-body rums were produced here in a column still. After the distillery was closed, the auction of the stock planned by the state was never held. Luckily, because independent bottlers and cask traders could buy the casks and store them in Europe – in some cases up until today. The bottling from the Caroni stock is among the most sought-after and expensive bottles on the market.

### Caroni 1998 Bristol Spirits

*John Barrett from Bristol Spirits is one of the fillers who makes the heritage of the closed distillery accessible to us very knowledgeably. This rum is complex, heavy, and still a little untamed.*

### Caroni 1974 Bristol Spirits

*Only few bottles are still available worldwide from this vintage. Here you can find the whole complexity of Caroni in one bottle. A sensational rum, which succeeds in having an aroma of sweet sultanas and burning car tyres at the same time.*

### Caroni 1984–2006 Full-proof Velier

*Luca Gargano from the Italian bottler has brought many different Caronis onto the market. Almost each individual one is unsurpassed and Velier is the benchmark for all things in this area. Unfortunately, also unsurpassed in terms of prices, insofar as bottles can still be found at all. His Caroni from the year 1984 was one of the most fascinating, but also most untypical that I have ever sampled.*

### Caroni 1997–2015 Liquid Art
🍾🍾🍾🍾 / 🎲 / ♨ / 📇

This bottling comes from the small Belgian bottler Liquid Art. A typical represent-ative, but a little lighter and fruitier than other Caronis.

### Caroni 1997–2011 Silver Seal
🍾🍾🍾🍾🍾 / 🎲🎲 / ♨ / 📇

The bottler Silver Seal comes from the number one rum-loving country – Italy. However, the casks are stored in Glasgow. A heavy, complex rum with great strength.

### Caroni 1997–2015 A. D. Rattray
🍾🍾🍾🍾🍾 / 🎲 / ♨ / 📇

Another 1997 Caroni – this one from the Scottish "whisky bottler" A. D. Rattray. Very direct and a little bit of a bite, but with a fully loaded "rubber taste".

# Rum & Coca Cola

If you ever go down Trinidad
They make you feel so very glad
Calypso sing and make up rhyme
Guarantee you one real good fine
time

Drinkin' rum and Coca-Cola
Go down Point Koomahnah
Both mother and daughter
Workin' for the Yankee dollar

Oh, beat it man, beat it

Since the Yankee come to Trinidad
They got the young girls all goin'
mad
Young girls say they treat 'em nice
Make Trinidad like paradise

Drinkin' rum and Coca-Cola
Go down Point Koomahnah
Both mother and daughter
Workin' for the Yankee dollar

Oh, you vex me, you vex me

From Chicachicaree to Mona's Isle
Native girls all dance and smile
Help soldier celebrate his leave
Make every day like New Year's Eve

Drinkin' rum and Coca-Cola
Go down Point Koomahnah
Both mother and daughter
Workin' for the Yankee dollar

It's a fact, man, it's a fact

In old Trinidad, I also fear
The situation is mighty queer
Like the Yankee girl, the native
swoon
When she hear der Bingo croon

Drinkin' rum and Coca-Cola
Go down Point Koomahnah
Both mother and daughter
Workin' for the Yankee dollar

Out on Manzanella Beach
G. I. romance with native peach
All night long, make tropic love
Next day, sit in hot sun and cool off

Drinkin' rum and Coca-Cola
Go down Point Koomahnah
Both mother and daughter
Workin' for the Yankee dollar

It's a fact, man, it's a fact

Rum and Coca-Cola
Rum and Coca-Cola
Workin' for the Yankee dollar

*Lord Invader, 1942*

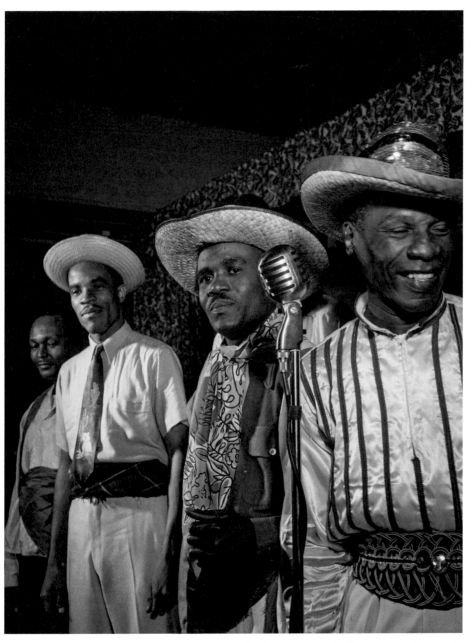

*Presumably in the Renaissance Ballroom, Harlem 1947*
*Second from right: Lord Invader (Photo: William P. Gottlieb)*

*Worthy Park Estate, Jamaica (Photo: Worthy Park)*

# JAMAICA

Jamaica is the country with the greatest bar density in the world – a statistic that does not even include the illegal joints. A lot is therefore drunk in Jamaica and rum is no small part of it. Apart from reggae and the Rastafarian ideology, the country is known for Jamaica rum, especially in Germany. In the 18th century, very high import duties were applied to foreign spirits, which is why rum was cut with German neutral alcohol and water. Up until today, these mixes must only contain 5 percent of Jamaica rum, which keeps the import levies low and has led to the name "Jamaica rum cut". This rum was ideally suited to it, as the Jamaicans know better than all others how to distil so-called high-ester rum: extremely concentrated, highly aromatic rum. In a pure form, it is said to be rather unpalatable, but it is perfectly suited to cutting.

A very important step when making this type of rum is fermentation. In Jamaica, "dunder" and "skimming" are traditionally added here. Dunder is the liquid that remains in the pot still after the distilling process (slop). It is gathered in a deep and rather unappetising dunder pit outdoors. Due to the open storage in the sun, the pH value of the slop is reduced. By adding it to molasses, the value decreases further and therefore creates an environment in which yeast fungus works best. This system was originally introduced to stabilize quality. The American bourbon producers do the same – here the process is called "sour mash".

Skimming is the foam that deposits on the surface in sugar manufacturing when simmering the sugarcane juice. It helps to start fermentation and has, like the dunder, a strong influence on the typical flavour of Jamaica rum.

This style is also called "Continental Flavoured Rum" or "German Style" in Jamaica. After this there come the somewhat less intensive styles "Wedderburn", "Plummer", and "Common Clean" – graded according to the ester content (aldehydes) in the rum.

This all sounds (and is) a bit complicated but it opens up a wide spectrum of combinations of different styles. However, in any variant, Jamaica rum is aromatic and very characteristic. With 10 million litres per year, the British colony Jamaica was the largest rum producer in the world at the end of the 18th century.

At the time, there were 18,300 British inhabitants to 226,000 slaves. With the Slavery Abolition Act, with which the British Parliament abolished slavery throughout the Empire in 1834, the decline of the Jamaican sugar and rum industry started, which did not however affect the quality of the drink.

## National Rums of Jamaica Limited (NRJ)

In this special case, this is not a distillery but a company that currently owns three distilleries. It was founded in 2006, also to preserve the heritage of Jamaican rum production. Of formerly many hundred distilleries, only six are still active today. NRJ belongs in equal parts to the state of Jamaica, the Demarara Distillers from Guyana and the West Indies Rum Distillery from Barbados, which in turn has belonged to the French cognac producer Maison Ferrand since 2017 – and therefore also its shares in NRJ. The three distilleries of NRJ are Clarendon, Inswood, and Long Pond – whereby Clarendon is currently the only one that really distils rum. To make it all even more complicated, NRJ only owns 73 percent of Clarendon, the rest belongs to the major spirits corporation Diageo. Production takes place at Clarendon, aging and bottling at Inswood. At Long Pond, on the other hand, there are large volumes of stored rum, which makes the distillery very valuable.

# Clarendon Distillery (Monymusk Distillery)

What we call the Clarendon Distillery today are actually two distilleries. The Monymusk Distillery opened in 1949 now houses two big pot stills and their fermentation tanks. 3 million litres (100 % alc. vol.) of heavy rum are produced here per year.

The new, enormous column still plant that produced 75 percent of the output at Clarendon was put into operation in 2009 – supported by a few million from the European Union. The Jamaican prime minister inaugurated it personally. Alcohol is distilled for many different purposes here. The main buyer, however, is the spirits corporation Diageo. As mentioned above, they hold a minimum share in Clarendon. The main reason for this are the two brands Captain Morgan and Myers Rum. Nearly 90 percent of production is said to flow into these two brands!

Monymusk rum is also the main brand of NRJ in Jamaica. In Europe, however, one can find bottles almost only from independent bottlers.

## Captain Morgan Spiced Rum

Captain Morgan is the embodiment of spiced rum worldwide. As its alcohol content is less than 37.5 %, in most countries it is officially not rum, which is why it is not listed here. Although a large proportion of the alcohol distilled at Clarendon is for this product, it is only for the European market. The largest proportion is produced in St. Croix (U. S. Virgin Islands), as the corporation benefits there from tax relief for the U. S. market. Diageo does not hold the rights to the name Captain Morgan in one country: in Jamaica. Here the rum by this name belongs to the company Wray & Nephews and is therefore one of the largest competitors of Diageo – Campari. Of course, they distil their own Captain Morgan rum, but which is only available in Jamaica.

## Monymusk 9yo W. D. J. Marketing
🍾🍾🍾🍾 / 🎲🎲 / 🍵 / 🗄

*W. D. J. Marketing was a British bottler that has not been around for a long time, but some of the bottling can still be found. A very classical representative of the heavy Jamaican style. A complex, impressive rum.*

## Long Pond Distillery

The sugar factory and the distillery can look back on a very long tradition. It was opened back in 1753. The sugar factory now belongs to Everglades Farms (Hampden Distillery). The Long Pond Distillery, on the other hand, is owned by NRJ and has had many changes of ownership over the years. Until Captain Morgan also entered the scene here: this brand was launched in 1944 by Seagram's. The corporation used rum for this from different distilleries of the Trelawny Parish, an area where rum and sugar-cane are deeply rooted. Seagram's was able to acquire Long Pond in 1953. In 1977 there was another change of owner – Long Pond now belonged to the state of Jamaica, who sold it again in 1993 to a consortium of finance enterprises and individuals. When NRJ was then founded in 2006, Long Pond together with Clarendon and Inswood came to their current owner, who closed the distillery in 2012, but then reopened it in July 2017. The new co-owner Maison Ferrand had probably exerted its influence.

Long Pond possesses five pot stills from the manufacturers Vendome and John Dore, which are all to be reactivated in the medium term, along with two column stills, which however will not continue running.

## *Vale Royal 2002 9 yo Bristol Spirits*

🍾🍾🍾🍾 / ▨▨ / ♨ / ⚗

*A lovely bottling by Bristol Spirits, which has been allowed to mature for nine years. Its name refers to the distillery Vale Royal that was in the immediate neighbourhood of Long Pond and was also bought by Seagram's in 1955 to run it together with Long Pond. The typical aromas of overripe fruits are very well incorporated here.*

## *Jamaica 1982 Flying no. 11 30 yo*

🍾🍾🍾🍾🍾 / ▨ / ♨ / ⚗

*A striking explosion of aromas by the Danish bottler Juuls Vin & Spiritis and a very sought-after one at that. Unfortunately, there are only 186 bottles of it. The extreme aromas are very well incorporated and the aftertaste is endless.*

# J. Wray & Nephew Ltd.

John Wray owned a taverna in Kingston in the second half of the 19th century and distilled his own rum for it. When his nephew Charles J. Ward entered the company, they started to distil and blend rum on a larger scale. They soon won the first three gold medals at the Great London Exhibition. In 1916 the Wrays also acquired Appleton and thereby became the largest producer in Jamaica. Today Wray & Nephew is an institution in Jamaica. The company owns the Appleton Estate, which was first mentioned in 1655. The distillery verifiably produced rum for the first time in 1749. It is here that the rums of the Appleton Line are produced, on five enormous pot stills and a column system.

The other active distillery that now belongs to the group is the New Yarmouth Estate.

In addition, there is the Holland Estate sugar factory. With these distilleries, apart from the Appleton and Wray & Nephew rums, they also produce for the Basel company Coruba or the Blackwell rum of the music producer of the same name, who once helped to spread reggae music in the world. Since 2012 Wray & Nephews has belonged to the Italian Gruppo Campari.

### Wray & Nephew Overproof
🍾🍾🍾🍾 / ⬛⬛⬛ / 🍯 / ⚗️ & 🏭

*In Jamaica this rum is drunk on every street corner – often like water, sometimes with water. A ratio of 1:4 is recommended, but try it yourself. This cleanly distilled rum can also be enjoyed pure or on ice – at least for those who like it strong. It remains open as to which distilling apparatus of which distillery the proportions of Wray & Nephew come from exactly. The New Yarmouth Estate, however, is supposed to have a significant influence.*

### Appleton 12 yo
🍾🍾🍾🍾 / ⬛⬛⬛ / 🍯 / ⚗️ & 🏭

*At least twelve years in various casks (bourbon, cognac, sherry, wine) give this powerful rum plenty of refinement. The Appleton rums also contain rum from the column still, alongside the pot-still distillates typical of Jamaica. This makes it somewhat lighter and more accessible. However, it still never conceals its origins.*

### Appleton 21 yo
🍾🍾🍾🍾 / ⬛⬛⬛ / 🍯 / ⚗️ & 🏭

*The top product by Appleton. Stored for at least twenty-one years in little oak and sherry casks. Everything very balanced, round, and full. A great rum.*

### Appleton Joy

🍶🍶🍶🍶 / 🎲🎲🎲 / 🍯 / 🧪 & 🗄

For her twenty-year anniversary as a "master blender" at Appleton, Joy Spence was allowed to create this rum. The casks she used have a maturation time of between twenty-five and thirty-five years behind them. The pot-still elements are very clear in the nose, but more palatable than expected.

### Appleton 50 yo

🍶🍶🍶🍶 / 🎲🎲 / 🍯 / 🧪 & 🗄

Launched in 2012, for the 50$^{th}$ anniversary of Jamaica's independence, and officially the rum with the world's longest cask-storage. A blend of three "surviving" sherry casks, with a bottle priced at around 4,400 Euros. I was able to sample this rum at its market launch. What is fascinating is that it is still very palatable even after fifty years in sherry casks. However, its price is due more to its rarity and its age than its complexity.

### New Yarmouth 2005 12 yo / Cave Guildive

🍶🍶🍶🍶🍶 / 🎲 / 🍯 / 🧪

The New Yarmouth Sugar Estate was mentioned for the first time at the beginning of the 18$^{th}$ century. The rum distillery of the same name works both with column- and pot-still apparatus. Their output is supposedly greater than that of Appleton. A significant component of the unmistakable taste of Wray & Nephew's overproof is thought to be due to this distillery. Otherwise little can be found out about it and since it has belonged to the Gruppo Campari, no more individual casks are sold. This single cask by the Zurich bottler Cave Guildive is pure pot-still rum and therefore very intensive. Typical Jamaica: aromas of flax and smoke are coupled with the typical overripe fruits with a very long aftertaste.

## Hampden Estate

Earlier over a hundred distilleries line the north coast of Jamaica. Apart from the Long Pond Distillery, only Hampden Estate has survived. In 2003 the distillery was nationalized and then closed shortly afterwards. The Hussey family, the owner of the company Everglades Farms, bought it in 2009 to put it back into operation. Hampden is known for producing a very rich rum, which often reaches Europe as a cut rum. Here there are no column stills, but just four pot stills from three different manufacturers. For some time, they have had the rum Fire on the market as their own white "overproof" product, and with Hampden Gold also a 40% golden rum. Both are intended more for use in cocktails.

Alongside this, under the direction of the Hussey family, rum started to be stored in casks. Until 2010, the whole production was sold to Europe as so-called "bulk rum" – meaning open. This means all the older bottling by Hampden has been stored in Europe, and not an insignificant amount either. Certain old "single cask" bottles have a very high value today among collectors.

*Mr. Buchanan, Christelle Harris, and Mr. Mackenzie (Photo: Hampden Estate)*

### *Hampden Estate Gold Rum*
🍾🍾🍾🍾 / ⬛⬛ / 🍶 / ⚗️

*The storage for several years and the low alcohol percentage make it relatively mellow and it can also be drunk pure. It remains, however, a very good rum for powerful cocktails and punches.*

### *Hampden 8yo Cadenhead's*
🍾🍾🍾🍾🍾 / ⬛ / 🍶 / ⚗️

*The bottler Cadenhead's has repeatedly brought old Hampden rums onto the market that were allowed to mature slowly in Scotland. This rum comes from the time before the closure of the distillery.*
*Undiluted and in full cask strength, the whole almost stark, aromatic diversity of Jamaica flows into the glass. Extremely intense and very strong – this rum can be diluted with some water without a guilty conscience.*

### *Hampden 1993–2016 Cave Guildive*
🍾🍾🍾🍾🍾 / ⬛ / 🍶 / ⚗️

*This is a very intensive Jamaican rum. For those who do not like it, it is reminiscent of nail varnish remover. But those whom it suits rave about its endless and ever-changing aftertaste.*

## Worthy Park

When the distilling furnaces were shut down in 1960, this "sugar estate" could look back on 220 years of rum production. Well into the next century, the focus was then put on sugar production and they established one of the most efficient factories in the Caribbean. In 2005 Gordon Clarke, whose family has owned the estate for four generations, saw an opportunity to rebuild the distillery. Two years later, the first "new" Worthy Park Rum was bottled – a white, strong "overproof rum" as is popular in Jamaica. Worthy Park only owns one pot still from Forsyths in Scotland. It can produce a quantity of 12,000 bottles of overproof rum per day. This estate prides itself on the fact that everything is done in-house from the sugar-cane shoot to the finished and stored rum. Whereas this was usual in the past, today it is rather an exception.

### Rum-Bar Rum overproof

*This white 65 strong classic Jamaica rum is blended out of three different distinct qualities. However, as it is purely from the pot still, it comes across as very powerful. Although the distillery has only been making rum again since 2007, it creates the impression of always having been there.*

### Worthy Park Single Estate Reserve

*This rum, stored for six to eight years, is relatively new on the market. It is the first that the distillery has brought onto the market under their name. Apart from its clear pot-still flavour, there are also ample fruity and somewhat lighter hints. Very accomplished.*

*Worthy Park Estate, Jamaica (Photo: Worthy Park)*

# ST. LUCIA

The pirate François Le Clerc, called "Jambe de Bois" (Wooden Leg), was the first European to settle on St. Lucia. Owing to the volcanic mountain landscape and the impenetrable rainforest, the Caribs were able to successfully resist the competing colonial powers here. The island therefore remained for a long time a pirates' nest and attempts to settle failed repeatedly. In 1605, for example, sixty-seven Englishmen were stranded in St. Lucia on the way to Guyana. After a month on the island, only nineteen were still alive and fled in a canoe. St. Lucia was occupied fourteen times alternately by France and Great Britain, until it was allocated definitively to the British Crown in 1814. Queen Elisabeth II is still the head of state today. Petit and Grand Piton, the two volcanoes, whose flanks in the west jut directly into the sea, are UNESCO world heritage sites and therefore countless cruise ships pass by here. Despite this, the island has been able to preserve its charm of past times, with weekly dance events on the street and little shacks where a rum mixed with roots, herbs, and spices is drunk. Of the former three distilleries, only one remains and the sugarcane plantations have been superseded by bananas. For this reason, today the molasses is imported from Guyana and the Dominican Republic, although this does not diminish the very good quality of the rum.

## St. Lucia Distillers Ltd

The St. Lucia Distillers Ltd. was founded in 1972. It is a merger of Geest Industries and the Barnard family, who ran two distilleries in Roseau and Dennery. The technical equipment was pooled and installed in a new distillery in Roseau. Lorrie Barnard ran the distillery from 1972 to his death in 2012 in a very innovative manner and twenty-five different products were manufactured here. Since the year 2016, the distillery belongs to the Groupe Bernard Hayot that is at home on Martinique.
To be able to produce a wide range of rum styles, it works with a double-column-still facility and three different pot stills.

## Chairman's Reserve

🍶🍶🍶 / ▢▢ / 🍯 / ⚗🍾 & 🛢

*This rum contains components from all distilling equipment at the distillery. They are developed separately in bourbon casks from Jim Beam, Jack Daniels, and Buffalo Trace and are only amalgamated after at least five years. A very balanced, perfectly made medium-body rum.*

## Chairman's Reserve The Forgotten Casks

🍶🍶🍶 / ▢▢▢ / 🍯 / ⚗🍾 & 🛢

*In 2007, large sections of the distillery in Roseau were destroyed in a fire. As warehouses also burnt down, the casks were stored elsewhere on the island. Some of the casks were forgotten for up to five years. This unfortunate circumstance resulted in a more intensive, somewhat sweeter variant of the Chairman's Reserve.*

## Secret Treasures Selection Privée Vendome 6 yo

🍶🍶🍶🍶 / ▢▢ / 🍯 / ⚗

*The bottler Secret Treasures once belonged to the Swiss company Fassbind and was taken over in 2005 by the German trader Haromex. This six-year rum comes from the Vendome Still, which was put into operation in 2003. The rum is very heavy and aromatic, but with beautiful fruity tones.*

### Secret Treasures Selection Privée John Dore 9 yo

🍾🍾🍾🍾 / ▢▢ / ♨ / ⚗

This rum comes from one of two pot stills from the manufacturer John Dore. It is somewhat less fruity than the one described above, but almost a little smoky. With these two single-still bottlings it is clear why even the official blended rums of St. Lucia Distillers are so accomplished. These three pot stills simply result in a lovely fruity-heavy rum.

# GRENADA

Grenada enjoys the nickname "Spice Island" in the Caribbean. It is famous for its excellent cocoa beans and nutmeg. On the island there is also rum spiced with nutmeg, which, however, is not widely available abroad. However, Grenada also cultivates sugarcane and in the past it was home to some exciting distilleries, but which have unfortunately almost all closed down today. At La Sagesse one can still visit the dilapidated equipment. Westerhall Estate does not distil itself anymore and the over 200-year-old Dunfermline Rum Distillery did not survive Hurricane Ivan in the year 2004. Classical pot stills were mostly used here for distilling directly from sugarcane juice. A very interesting style that has otherwise more or less died out. At least with River Antoine one of the most exciting distilleries worldwide is still in operation. It distils in the same way as was usual in Grenada back in the 18th century.

## Westerhall Estate

Rum was produced here from 1800. The distillery has now unfortunately been disused for quite a long time. The white rum comes from Trinidad and is blended on the estate, stored in casks and bottled. The Williams family, who owns the estate, also plants cocoa, citrus fruits, bananas, and sugarcane. In the year 2017, the family sold parts of the company. Together with the new co-owners, there are serious plans to refurbish the distillery and put it into operation. Mark Reynier, who has already revitalized the Bruichladdich Distillery in Scotland, is also involved in this project.

*Street scene in Sauters, Grenada*

## Westerhall Rum No. 5
🍾🍾🍾 / ⬜⬜⬜ / ♨ / 📖

*The No. 5 is a so-called "sipping rum", with at least five years in the cask, which means it is intended to be drunk pure. In the nose it is still slightly alcoholic, in the mouth very mild and smooth – but with a strong character.*

## Westerhall Rum No. 10
🍾🍾🍾 / ⬜⬜⬜⬜ / ♨ / 📖

*The flagship of the range has been stored for ten years in oak casks. It is full-bodied, very mild, and balanced.*

## River Antoine Distillery

The River Antoine Distillery should actually be declared a UNESCO world heritage site immediately. It was built in 1785 and has hardly changed since then. Electricity is only available in the office, otherwise it is powered with water power, wood, or "bagasse", the dried remains of the squashed sugarcane. The mighty water wheel is labelled with the year mentioned above and drives the sugarcane press, as well as a conveyor belt that is just as old. Then the juice flows into the "concentration room", where it is heated increasingly in five sequential basins through the burning bagasse. In a sixth basin, the juice is mixed with 5 to 10 percent of molasses (for sweetening) and then fermented openly for eight days. In recent years, this no longer happens in casks, but in concrete tanks, the only major innovation in 250 years.

Distilling happens in two pot stills fired by wood, with two attached boosters. The rum thus achieves a minimum alcohol content of 75%. If not, it goes back to be distilled again. Once 75% has been reached, it is bottled and sold locally immediately. There is also a 69% version for tourists – because rum with an alcohol content of over 70% may not be transported on planes.

*Ruins of a sugar mill, Grenada*

### *Rivers Royale Grenadian Rum*

This rum is unique in the rum world: distilled from pure juice extracted from hand-cut local sugarcane in ancient pot stills, with 5 to 10 percent of molasses – and all of this fully "overproof". I have never encountered this combination and it evokes highly dubious backyard distilleries. However, it was once typical of Grenada rum. The result is scarcely palatable for spoiled Central European rum drinkers and in the first moment it is reminiscent of lighter fuel, brush cleaner, or nail varnish remover. There is perhaps no other rum that comes as close to the pirate schnapps of the past that is steeped in myth. However, those who get used to it find some pleasant fruity notes. The extremely high alcohol content is also less present than might be feared. This rum is nevertheless recommended on ice, which may melt a little. In the north of Grenada, a "Rivers" is an absolute must for the local population and a synonym for rum in general. A local, with whom I drank Rivers during a visit to Grenada, hit the nail on the head: "It's the best rum in the world but it stinks." Unfortunately, it is almost never available in Europe, but I am working on it.

*(The pictures on the two inner sides of the cover show the distillery.)*

68

*The "concentration room" at River Antoine, Grenada*

## Grenada Distillers Ltd

The biggest distillery on Grenada has been producing rum since 1937. It is distilled in a column-still facility. The unusual feature at Clarke's Court Rum, however, is that they distil molasses, sugarcane juice, and sugar syrup – depending on what happens to be available. The motto here therefore, as so often in the Caribbean, is: if there is something, then take it. Already tomorrow there may be nothing left.

### *Clarke's Court Old Grog*

*The Old Grog is the premium rum from Clarke's Court. In this case, grog does not refer to the cocktail of the same name, but to the old lettering on casks. The former king of England, George III, is supposed to have received the best rums from Grenada. The casks were labelled with G. R. O. G. – Georgius Rex Old Grenada. The present-day Grog rum is very palatable, with strong aromas of tropical fruits and a good sweetness.*

# ANTIGUA

In 1632 the British settled in Antigua and remained the colonial power until the declaration of independence in 1981. After that, Antigua formed a confederation with the islands Barbuda and Redonda. In the south lies the so-called English Harbour. The former naval port of the Royal Navy is one of the few harbours safe from tropical storms owing to its natural location and it also gave the local rum its name.

It has only had its own rum distillery since 1932. Before that, rum was imported from Barbados, bottled by the local "rum shops" and partly also mixed with sugar or plum juice. The owners of these "rum shops" were often Portuguese from Madeira, who knew a thing or two about rum.

## Antigua Distillery Ltd.

Seven of the eight founders of this distillery were rum shop owners with Portuguese roots. The French Savalle quadruple column still installed at the time was replaced in 1991 by a threefold copper one from John Dore. In the beginning, the distillery only sold open rum to local traders. They called what was stored Caballero, which later became the Cavalier rum that still exists today. With the new column facility, they also created a premium segment – these rums are called "English Harbour" after the famous harbour.

### *English Harbour 10 yo*

*Matured for at least ten, but partially also up to twenty-five years in little oak casks. A solid, sweetish, medium-body rum.*

# BRITISH VIRGIN ISLANDS (TORTOLA)

Rum is part of the history and tradition on the thirty little islands of the British Virgin Islands. Memories of the rum-drenched days of the marines are still alive here.

From 1680 England took definitive control again over the islands, after a brief intermezzo with the Netherlands. The British continued what the Dutch had started: planting sugar and producing rum. On the main island Tortola, some distillates still emerge that are strong and wild, contrary to the neighbouring St. Croix rum. Unfortunately, it is practically never available in our latitudes.

## Pusser's West Indies Ltd.

Because in the past the drinking water on ships was often dirtied, the bacteria in the water were neutralized with rum. Admiral Edward Vernon (nickname "Old Grog") ordered that the quarter of a litre per day given to the crew be divided into two rations, diluted with water and – against the vitamin-deficiency disease scurvy – that a slice of lemon be added. This heralded the invention of grog (page 194). For over 300 years, each sailor of the Royal Navy received his daily ration of rum from the so-called "pusser", the numbers and provisions master (from "purse"). This practice was abolished on 31 July 1970, the Black Death Day still wistfully celebrated today. As a replacement, a fund was set up for seamen – the Royal Navy Sailors' Fund, called "Death Fund" in the vernacular.

In the year 1979, Charles Tobias was able to buy and commercialize the original recipe. A requirement that still applies today are financial donations to the "Death Fund". Pusser's rum is the largest income source of the fund today and Charles Tobias has since also been honoured by the Queen for his services.

Now the headquarters of Pusser's is in the U.S.A. and bottling takes place in Guyana. However, in this book I will leave it on the Virgin Islands, as this is where everything started and for a long time blending and bottling took place here.

## *Pusser's Rum*
🍶🍶🍶🍶 / ▨▨▨ / 🍥 / 🗄 & 📑

*The rum is still made according to a secret recipe and is a cut of five different rums from Guyana and Trinidad. The backbone has always been formed by proportions from the last two still existing wooden pot stills. Today they stand at the Demerara Distillery in Guyana.*
*It is very strong and spicy, but sweeter than the nose might expect. The company's self-promotion is "the single malt of rum", which is rather fitting.*

## *Nelson's Blood*
🍶🍶🍶🍶 / ▨▨▨▨ / 🍥 / 🗄 & 📑

*A Pusser's Rum that has been stored at least fifteen years in casks and is therefore a little sweeter and smoother. The name comes from a rather unappetising seaman story. When Admiral Nelson fell in the Battle of Trafalgar in 1805, his corpse was brought to London to enable a state burial. To ensure the corpse arrived well-preserved, it is said to have been laid in a rum cask. The seamen were rightly outraged that now too little rum was left for them and they drilled the cask in secret. The rum that they now drank in secret allegedly had a reddish gold colour. It has been proven today that Nelson was "preserved" not in a rum cask, but in a brandy cask. The rum may still bear this name nevertheless.*

# U.S. VIRGIN ISLANDS (ST. CROIX)

The present-day American Virgin Islands belong to the larger western group of these islands. They have a chequered history behind them, as no fewer than seven nations have hoisted their flags here one after the other: Spain, England, Netherlands, France, Malta, Denmark, and finally the U.S.A., who purchased the territory in 1917 for 25 million dollars. Rum production started in the early 17$^{th}$ century with the French and then gained importance with the first British planters on the island St. Croix. The style at the time is said to have been very similar to the heavy Jamaican rum and enjoyed great esteem. Today the Cruzan rums (the name refers to the inhabitants of St. Croix) have a rather light, elegant body that is reminiscent of the Spanish style. Since 2011, Diageo has also been producing a large proportion of its approximately 90 million litres of Captain Morgan rum a year here in a specially built distillery.

## Cruzan Rum Distillery

This distillery is one of the largest in the Caribbean and is run by the Nelthropp family. Various multinational drink corporations have already come in and out as owners. Since 2008 the distillery has been owned by the U.S. company Beam Suntory.

Rum has been distilled here since 1760. Only once were the machines halted – during the prohibition in the U.S.A. As the last sugar mill on St. Croix was also closed, the molasses today comes from other countries. The rum made with it is very clean and rather light.

## Cruzan Single Cask

🍾🍾 / ▢▢▢ / 🍯 / 🏭

The single cask is a cut of various rums matured up to twelve years, which are brought together in a big new oak cask.

## A. H. Riise xo Reserve

🍾🍾 / ▢▢▢▢▢ / 🍯 / 🏭

In the 1837, Albert Heinrich Rüse received an exclusive licence to open a kind of pharmacy on the island St. Thomas belonging to Denmark. His business developed splendidly and soon he was also producing prize-winning "bay rum" – an aftershave on a rum basis, mixed with Caribbean bay leaf. The business has changed owners several times, but still exists and is today an enormous duty-free mall with thousands of articles.

The rum produced under Rüse's name is probably distilled at the Cruzan distillery and is an example of an extremely strongly sugared rum. Very sweet and with strong orange aromas.

# ANGUILLA

In Anguilla, the governor represented the British monarch Queen Elisabeth II as the head of state. The island is a so-called British overseas territory. The inhabitants live primarily from luxury tourism, lobster fishing, and offshore banking. Until the foundation of the Anguilla Rum Company, sugar and rum were of no major importance on this island.

## Anguilla Rum Company

The Anguilla Rum Company was not founded until 1995 with the aim of offering rum in the premium sector. There is no distillery, the producers blend rums from various origins.

### *Pyrat XO Reserve Planters Gold*

🪔 / 🎲🎲🎲🎲🎲 / 🍂 / 🎹

*A liqueur-like, very sweet rum with strong orange aromas and a lot of added sugar.*

# BERMUDA

Bermuda is also a British overseas territory. The first European to come across the island was the Spaniard Juan de Bermúdez in 1503, but he did not even go ashore due to the dangerous reefs. Then in 1609, 150 English colonialists ran aground on one of these reefs and so became the first involuntary settlers. Today Bermuda lives especially off tourism and its reputation as a tax haven. Many international companies have relocated their official base there, such as Bacardi, in a very beautiful Mies van der Rohe house. There is neither sugarcane nor a distillery here, but even so the national rum Gosling's Black Seal is the most important export product in terms of volume.

## Gosling Brothers Ltd.

In the year 1806, James Gosling landed on Bermuda – he no longer had enough money for the crossing to America. Together with his brother, he opened a shop in the capital Hamilton in 1824. When James went back to London his brother Ambrose continued running the shop, but it was only his sons who started to blend and sell rum in 1857. Until the First World War, Gosling was available only from the cask. Their Black Seal then became world-famous with the cocktail Dark & Stormy, to which Gosling owns the name copyright.

### Gosling's Black Seal
🎍🎍 / 🀫🀫🀫🀫 / 🍶 / 🧴

*A cut of three separately matured rums from the Caribbean. The rum is cut and bottled in Bermuda, but not manufactured. The only permitted rum for Bermuda's official national cocktail of rum, ginger beer, and a slice of lime is Black Seal, without which it may not be called Dark & Stormy. Only of limited suitability to be enjoyed pure.*

*Havana, Cuba*

# CUBA

Cuba formerly covered a third of the world's requirement of cane sugar. It is only logical, therefore, that a lot of rum has always been distilled here. The Cuban Facundo Bacardí is attributed the honour of having driven the wickedness out of rum that it was associated with for a long time. By means of filtration through activated charcoal, his rum became mild and light and blazed a successful trail in the form of cocktails. Almost all the classics come from Cuba. As the local rum is not very aromatic, it is very well suited to fruity and fresh Cuban cocktails.

During the time of the prohibition, many Americans travelled to Cuba to indulge in the sweet pleasures of life. One bar after another was opened – and while the bar culture was dying in the U.S.A., it was gaining strength in Cuba. An expression of this was the Club de Cantineros – a legendary association of Cuban barkeepers. It was intended to strengthen and honour the trade. For the first time in the history of bar culture, cocktails were mixed primarily with rum here. Later, Hemingway drank a vast number of daiquiris and mojitos in bars such as the Floridita or the Bodeguita del Medio.

There are still large distilleries on the island, but it is very difficult to visit them and find out more about them. As the market is dominated by Havana Club, many products never reach as far as Europe.

## Havana Club International

The first rum with the name Havana Club came onto the market in 1935 – it was distilled and launched as a branch at the distillery of José Arechabala, which had stood in Cárdenas since 1878. After the revolution by Fidel Castro and his fellow campaigners, the company was expropriated and the family, as well as the Bacardís, fled into exile. The name rights went to the Cuban state in 1973.

In 1993 the company Pernod Ricard entered a joint venture with the Cuban state and launched the rum worldwide (with the exception of the U.S.A), very much to the displeasure of the market leader Bacardi, which after years of legal disputes now sells a rum in the U.S.A that is also called

Havana Club and is produced in Puerto Rico, as is some of Bacardi itself. Havana Club represents the typical Cuban style very well. It is light, gentle, and a bit sweetish.

### *Havana Club Añejo 7 Años*

🍾 / ❄❄❄❄ / 🍮 / 🍶

*Very good, mild, dark rum for mixing or drinking pure.*

### *Havana Club Màximo extra añejo*

🍾 / ❄❄❄❄ / 🍮 / 🍶

*The "super premium rum" of the brand. A blend from the best casks. A bottle costs around 1,800 Euros – for which one gets an abundant woody taste.*

## Destilería Paraíso (Sancti Spíritus)

This distillery is in fact called Paraíso, but usually only called Sancti Spíritus, named after the town in the centre of Cuba where it is situated. Its production includes the Santero and Mulata rum and is probably the only distillery that also sells whole casks to bottlers. As is the case for all Cuban distilleries, there is little other information available.

### *Fine Cuban Rum 2003 / Bristol Spirits*

🍾 / ❄❄❄ / 🍮 / 🍶

*The oak casks where the rum was stored for seven years made their way to Great Britain, where they were bottled by Bristol Spirits. A very pleasant rum. Quite dry for a Cuban rum.*

### *Sancti Spíritus 17 yo 62,2 % / Cadenhead's*

🏋🏋 / 🎲🎲 / 💩 / 🧴

*A single cask, bottled in cask strength by Cadenhead's, is among the best that there is from Cuba.*

*Sugarcane harvest, Cuba*

# DOMINICAN REPUBLIC

The island Hispaniola belongs to the Greater Antilles and has been divided into two states since colonial times. The larger is the Dominican Republic, the smaller is Haiti. Hispaniola was one of the first islands to cultivate sugarcane. The first sugar mill was in operation back in 1516. It is probable that a type of rum was already produced back then. Even so, the island is often overlooked today by rum drinkers, because rums from the Dominican Republic do not have any resounding names. This is also because Hispaniola, contrary to the other large sugar islands, never brought forth its own distinctive style. The three big rum producers – Brugal, Barcelo, and Bermúdez – were Spanish immigrants and therefore fostered the Spanish-Cuban style: gentle spirits matured in American oak, of a delicate elegance with a perceptible hint of wood.

Apart from the three distilleries, the company Oliver & Oliver is also based in the Dominican Republic. They blend rum from various sources and produce a wide range of simple, sweetish rums. They are very successful with their brands such as "Puntacana", "Opthimus", "Quorhum", or "Cubaney", and those are only the most well-known examples of their ample portfolio.

## J. Armando Bermúdez & Co.

This family enterprise has been producing since 1852 in the little mountain town of Santiago. It is well known on the island, even if the two other major companies are more present internationally.

### *Bermúdez Aniversario*

🍶 / ▨ ▨ ▨ ▨ / 🝄 / 🏛

*A very pleasant, elegant, and soft rum.*

# HAITI

The slave uprising of 1791 on Haiti led to the "first black republic" modelled on the French Revolution. Under the leadership of the national hero Toussaint Louverture, the insurgents fought against suppression by the colonial powers and against British, French, and Spanish troops. The colonial powers were concerned with good reason, as they had become rich owing to slavery. In 1794, France declared the end of slavery in Haiti and on 1 January 1804 the state gained independence. This came at a price, however: not only the life of Toussaint Louverture, who had died two years previously in French captivity in Pontarlier near the Swiss border. In addition, France demanded 150 million French francs to grant recognition – today that corresponds to 21 billion dollars. This is how one of the richest colonies became one of the poorest states: 80 percent of the population live below the breadline.

However, the fact that nowhere in the Caribbean more rum is drunk is due more to the fact that the drink, which is called "Clairin" here, is an important part of many voodoo ceremonies. It is the rum of the poor, which is still produced as it was 300 years ago. The Italian Luca Gargano, who has been experimenting with Clairin for a number of years, has counted 532 rudimentary distilleries.

## Rhum Barbancourt

Dupré Barbancourt from the Charente (the cognac region) brought cognac technology to the island in 1800. Up until today, a very fine rum made of sugarcane juice is made at the distillery he founded. It is first distilled in a steel column still and then in copper pot stills, or as they are called in this case, "alambic charentais". The rums are then matured in casks made of Limousin oak in various sizes (up to 70 hectolitres). According to old tradition, distillation only takes from December to May, as in this dry season the sugarcane has the highest sugar content.

### *Rhum Barbancourt 8 ans (5 stars)*
🍶🍶 / 🎲🎲🎲 / 🍫 / ⚗️ & 📇

*A very great rum with perfect balance – due to this Barbancourt is among the very important addresses.*

### *Rhum Barbancourt 15 ans (Réserve du Domaine)*
🍶🍶 / 🎲🎲🎲 / 🍫 / ⚗️ & 📇

*The fifteen-year Barbancourt only has very limited availability. It has great elegance with pleasant sweetness.*

## Distillerie Arawaks

Arawaks was the name of the original inhabitants of the Caribbean who were driven out by the European settlers. Danois Vaval, the father of the present-day owner Fritz, founded the distillery after the Second World War and named it in their honour. It was extensively removed in 2005, but still today, chemicals or additives have no place in Vaval's rum production.

### *Vaval*
🍶🍶🍶 / 🎲 / 🍫 / ⚗️ & 📇

*On one little pot still ("alambic") and one column still with eight trays, a very fresh rum is produced here with a very strong character.*

## Distillerie Douglas Casimir

Baradères, the little village where Casimir produces his Clairin, is so isolated that time seems to have stood still there. The same applies to the distillery that was founded by the father of the owner. The aromatic scent of the old type of sugarcane that grows in the area is enhanced further by adding aniseed, sorrel, or other spices.

### *Casimir*

🥃🥃🥃 / ▣ / 🍫 / 🍶 & 📖

*On a little pot still ("alambic") and a column still with six trays, a rum is produced here that is actually a spiced rum. However, it has nothing in common with the sticky drinks that are usually offered in this category. Extreme flavour!*

## Distillerie Chelo

The distillery Chelo is at 450 metres above sea level, on a high plateau amidst the mountains that can only be accessed along a track. The sugar comes from its own plantations and is an original variety that has otherwise disappeared from the Caribbean. It is harvested by hand and transported by mule. No chemical pesticides are used on the land owned by Michel Sajous. The Clairin Sajous is considered one of the most perfect versions of this rum from a past era.

### *Sajous*

🥃🥃🥃 / ▣ / 🍫 / 🍶 & 📖

*Production also takes place here on a little pot still ("alambic") and a column still with six trays. This is the "purest" of the four Clairins. If Haiti still belonged to France it would still be a true rhum agricole. This is because according to law, only rum produced on French territory may bear this name (which does not prevent Haitians from writing it on their label despite this).*

## Distillerie Bethel Romelus

In the northeast of Haiti lies the village of Pignon. The distillery owner Bethel Romelus works with "jus-cuit", which basically means boiled sugar-cane juice or sugarcane syrup. It is fermented spontaneously – fermentation starts without the addition of external yeast.

### *Le Rocher*

🍶🍶🍶🍶 / 🎲🎲 / 🌢 / 🍶 & 🗔

*This extremely aromatic rum is distilled on a pot still and then on a little column still. However, contrary to the other three Clairins, it has a very strong pot still aroma. Despite this, it still retains a very pleasant fruitiness. A very individual, wonderful rum of which there are not very many of its kind.*

# MARTINIQUE

In Martinique, rum is made almost exclusively out of sugarcane juice, the so-called rhum agricole. This was not always the case, as in the past nobody would have used this valuable raw product exclusively for alcohol. It started sometime between 1800 and 1820. When slavery was finally abolished in 1841, for many plantation owners it was no longer profitable to run a sugar factory. Many merged and produced sugar in a large factory. At the same time, more and more rum was distilled directly from the fermented juice of sugarcane.

Towards the end of the 19$^{th}$ century, a lot of rum was sold to the motherland France. The vine pest was raging at the time and wine became scarce. The demand for alcoholic drinks remained high, however, and the rum from the overseas territories experienced its heyday. Time passed by and wine made a return, and at the same time France was also producing more and more sugar from local sugarcane instead of importing it from the tropics. Faced with ruin, increasing numbers of sugar planters converted to distilling the rum directly from the sugarcane juice and gave up the unprofitable sugar production.

A clever decision, because today rhum agricole from Martinique is a famous top product subject to strict AOC regulations. These regulate the approved sugarcane types, the cultivation areas, the harvest periods and so on. The best producers are orientated towards the wine chateaux. They pay attention to vintages, terroir and the choice of casks.

The white rhums agricoles are earthy, vegetal, and a little sharp. A good white rhum agricole perfectly represents the sugarcane used, like a European fine brandy its fruit. It is perfectly suited to a Ti' Punch, a relative of the caipirinha and the daiquiri and the national drink on the French islands.

Through the cask storage, the rhums agricoles become very elegant and achieve a great complexity and variety of aromas. The best Martinique rums do not need to shy away from a comparison with the famous cognac. Contrary to the many popular rums from around the world, they are never sweetish, light, or mellow, but once you have acquired a taste for it, it will not let you go.

As many distilleries were closed in the last century, but whose brands live on, we are supplying a brief overview here or where the rums are distilled today. The choice of vat and storage have a very important influence here and in some distilleries there are even still the original distilling facilities from the old locations.

**Distillery of the Plantation Saint James:** Saint James/
Bally/Dillon/G. Hardy/Héritiers Madkaud
**Distillerie Depaz:** Depaz
**Distillerie La Mauny:** La Mauny / Trois Rivières/Duquesne
**Distillerie Neisson:** Neisson
**Distillerie Simon:** Saint Étienne (HSE)/Clément
**Distillerie J.M:** J.M
**Distillerie La Favorite:** La Favorite
**Habitation du Simon:** A1710
**Usine du Galion:** Grand Arôme/Grand Fond Galion

## Distillerie J.M

J.M is the smallest and northernmost distillery on Martinique and undoubtedly the most important address when it comes to mature rhums agricoles. The sugarcane comes exclusively from its own cultivation right near the distillery and the vats are all stored on site. They work very cleanly and with very good raw material – but the other great secrets that make this rum so unique will remain so.

### J. M vieux V. S. O. P:

🍾🍾🍾🍾 / ▢ / 🚬 / 📖

*At least four years in an oak cask. With ice, for cocktails, or pure.*

### J. M très vieux X. O.

🍾🍾🍾🍾 / ▢▢ / 🚬 / 📖

*At least six years in an oak cask. Pure as a digestif.*

### J. M très vieux 10 ans

🍾🍾🍾🍾 / ▢▢ / 🚬 / 📖

*At least ten-year-old rum bottled in vat strength ("brut de fut"). Always labelled with the year. One of the very great rums.*

### J. M très vieux 15 ans

🍾🍾🍾🍾 / ▢▢ / 🚬 / 📖

*At least fifteen-year-old rum bottled in vat strength ("brut de fut"). Always labelled with the year.*
*Over 70 percent of what once landed in the vat evaporates!*
*The fifteen-year-old J. M is for me one of the best rhums agricoles.*


## Distillery Depaz

In the little town of St. Pierre, which is situated right in the north of Martinique, there were once many distilleries. The flourishing town was considered "the Paris of the Caribbean". It is at the foot of the volcano Montagne Pelée, which erupted in 1902 and buried everything under its lava. Its fertile slopes are now the best ground for sugarcane, but even so almost all the distilleries relocated to safer places on the island after the catastrophe. Depaz is the only distillery that rebuilt everything – and is

*Distillery J. M, Martinique*

therefore the pride of the region. A very elegant, almost filigree rhum agricole is produced here, which alongside J. M is among the best Martinique has to offer.

## Depaz V. S. O. P.

🍾🍾🍾🍾 / 🎲🎲 / 🚬 / 🗃️

*Perfect, dry, very balanced rhum agricole with fine citrus notes.*

## Depaz X. O.

🍾🍾🍾🍾 / 🎲🎲 / 🚬 / 🗃️

*Twelve years in a little oak cask. Perfect. One of the great Martinique rums.*

## Plantation Saint James

On the slope on the other side of Montagne Pelée there was once the original St. James building that miraculously withstood the eruption of 1902 virtually without damage. Despite this, since 1974 production has taken place at the new site in Sainte-Marie. Saint James had the first square bottle in the world, which had many advantages for storage and packaging. The name was a deliberate anglophile choice, in order to have better chances on English-speaking markets. Although Saint James is a very large producer today, a lot is based on old traditions that go back to 1765. Since 1885, vintage bottling is undertaken here and at least six bottles of each of these bottles called "millésime" are stored in the cellar.

## Saint James 7 ans

🍾🍾🍾🍾 / 🎲🎲 / 🚬 / 🗃️

*The seven-year-old by Saint James still has the whole freshness of a young rhum agricole, but with wonderfully incorporated wood aromas from the cask. Very accomplished.*

92

## J. Bally

Square bottles are also used at J. Bally and here they are also proud of their tradition of millésime bottling. Distilling no longer takes place on the old site at Carbet, but at the Saint James distillery described above. The sugarcane, however, still comes from the old site. The rums are usually somewhat fruitier than those by Saint James.

### Bally Millésime 2000
🍶🍶🍶 / 🎲🎲 / 🚬 / 🧴

*Matured seven years in little cognac casks.*

## Distillery Dillon

Arthur Dillon was already a colonel in one of the Irish brigades under Louis XIV at the age of sixteen. He fought in the American War of Independence and landed in Martinique in 1779, where he married a cousin of the future empress and wife of Napoleon, Joséphine de Beauharnais. The sugar plantation that belonged to her family was given the name of Dillon and therefore also the rum. As the site is situated in Fort-de-France, the capital of Martinique, it was increasingly pressured by the growing town. Production has been closed down since 2006. The brand still exists, but today the majority of the rum comes from the Saint James distillery.

### Dillon V. S. O. P.
🍶🍶🍶 / 🎲🎲🎲 / 🚬 / 🧴

*A simple, but very well-made, somewhat sweetish rhum agricole.*

*Distilling column at Depaz, Martinique*

*Steel tanks at Depaz, Martinique*

# Habitation Clément

The distillery Habitation Clément and its beautiful park function today as a museum and tourist attraction. Their name is known throughout Martinique and those who visit the property can gain an impression of what wealth could once be made with sugar and rum. Today distilling takes place at the Distillerie du Simon, where the column-still facility of the burnt-down distillery Habitation Saint-Etienne also stands. However, Clément has enormous warehouses on his site with thousands of casks and offers a wide range of stored rum.

### Clément canne bleue
🍶🍶🍶 / ▨ / 🚬 / ▥

*Every year a new canne bleue vintage rum is brought onto the market at Clément. This is a white rhum agricole that is distilled exclusively from the juice of the sugarcane variety of the same name. Canne bleue is considered one of the finest types of sugarcane.*

### Clément 10 ans
🍶🍶🍶 / ▨▨ / 🚬 / ▥

*Perfectly matured, with a powerful hint of wood.*

# Habitation Saint Etienne (HSE)

The rums of the HSE brand are also distilled at the Distillerie du Simon in Le Francois, but on the original column stills from the burnt-down old distillery in Gros Morne. They are stored at the old site and in a wide variety of casks. HSE has made a name for itself in recent years by maturing its rum in varied casks, from single malt distilleries from Scotland to famous French wine cellars. Sometimes very interesting, but sometimes also a little arbitrary.

## HSE V. S. O. P.

🍶🍶🍶 / ▣▣ / 🚬 / ▥

*The classical rhum agricole by HSE is very accomplished. The V. S. O. P. matures in ex-bourbon and French oak casks and is a good, not very heavy rum with a sugarcane aroma.*

## Distillerie Neisson

Neisson is one of the few distilleries on Martinque that is still in family ownership. The brothers Jean and Arien Neisson founded it at the beginning of the 1930s and it is now run by Claudine Neisson-vernant. Neisson has the reputation of producing the best white rhum agricole, which is why even some of the stored qualities achieve an enormous price today. They exclusively use their own sugarcane, which is harvested by hand and is 60 percent of the fine canne bleue variety.

### Neisson blanc

🍶🍶🍶🍶 / ▣ / 🚬 / ▥

*The classic white rhum agricole is indeed very good. The aromas of freshly pressed sugarcane juice are perfectly captured.*

## Distillerie La Favorite

Rum has already been distilled here since 1851. At the beginning of the previous century, Henri Dormoy took over the distillery and installed modern equipment. The steam machine is still running today, while the distilling columns have changed often. Until his grandson, Paul Dormoy, last installed new copper columns in 2004, various distilling equipment stood here. Throughout the 1980s, for example, it was the columns of the Distillerie Saint-Etienne that now stand at the Distillerie du Simon. Today with Frank Dormoy, work is being carried out by the fourth generation to produce clean white rhum agricole. The stored rums do not have a very clear line and are of varying quality.

*La Favorite Coeur de Canne*

ᵭᵭᵭ / ⬡ / ✎ / ▥

*Good, clean rum with pleasant fruit aromas.*

# Habitation du Simon A1710

On 2 September 2016, another new distillery opened in Martinique, the Distillerie A1710. It was founded by Yves Assier de Pompignan, whose family moved to the island in 1710. The distillery is only a few hundred metres from the Distillerie du Simon that distils the rum for Clément and HSE. At A1710, however, distilling takes place on so-called alambic charentais – meaning the traditional little pot still that is used by cognac producers. Consequently, their own rum is not a rhum agricole according to strict AOC regulations, as it must then be produced on a column still. Even so, distilling is from the juice of local sugarcane that has been fermented for an untypically long period of five days. The aged rums of the Habitation du Simon are still acquired, but over the years their own will follow.

### *A1710 La Perle*

ᵭᵭᵭ / ⬡ / ✎ / ▤

*Their first own rum comes across as rather bulky. The yeast aromas are somewhat distinctive, but alongside this the sugarcane is also present. Unconventional but very interesting.*

*Old sugarcane train on the Saint James plantation, Martinique*

# GUADELOUPE

Like Martinique, Guadeloupe also belongs to France as an independent département. On the "île papillon" – its contours resemble a butterfly – simple Ti' Punch is drunk instead of Pastis. However, the success story of rum here is closely associated with another drink in the motherland: the first big upswing also occurred here with the French vine pest plague. The switch to rhum agricole was less radical though, so molasses rum is still created here today, but it does not enjoy such high esteem as the agricole products. In general, Guadeloupe is somewhat in the shadow of Martinique and its AOC system. They work according to the guidelines of an IGP system here – which is a little less strict. The rums from Guadeloupe usually have a bit less refinement, but are more full-bodied. Most distilleries are situated in Basseterre, the left wing of the butterfly that is covered with tropical rainforest. The flatter right part, Grande Terre, is a popular destination for French package tourists. The most important companies in the French Caribbean still belong today to the Békés, the white descendants of French settlers. Until today, they benefit from the wealth they achieved through slavery.

## Distillerie Damoiseau / Bellevue

The only remaining distillery on Grande Terre is Damoiseau – the largest and most well-known brand on Guadeloupe. It was founded in 1914 as Distillerie Bellevue and has been in the hands of the Damoiseaus since 1942. However, rum has only been filled into bottles since 1953. Apart from the well-known rum made of sugarcane juice, rum is also distilled from molasses here.

Unfortunately, the CEO of the distillery, Hervé Damoiseau, has often made headlines due to racist comments, provoking repeated boycotts against Damoiseau. He does not allow himself to be affected much by this. He is represented in more than forty countries worldwide with his rum and is therefore one of the most successful rhum agricole producers.

## Damoiseau 5 ans
🍾🍾🍾 / ▦▦ / 🍂 / 📇

*Like almost all rums by Damoiseau, the five-year-old is also rather light and simple in its flavour. The fact that these rums are not too extreme for anybody is probably also the secret of their success.*

## Distillerie Carrère (Montebello)
At Montebello near Petit-Bourg, they do not produce in the French standard style. Apart from using an untypical column facility, they also ferment significantly longer, which makes the distillates somewhat lighter than otherwise in Guadeloupe. The rhums agricoles are usually mixed with molasses rum, resulting in very interesting distillates. The distillery has existed since 1930 but was temporarily closed in the meantime (1960–1968).

## Montebello 6 ans
🍾🍾🍾 / ▦▦▦ / 🍂 & ☕ / 📇

*Stored at least six years in used bourbon casks. An easy to drink, but very good rum.*

## Distillerie Reimonenq (Musée du Rhum)
The two brothers who founded the Distillerie Reimonenq in 1916 had their roots in Scandinavia. To make the name a little more Francophone, they simply added on a "q". Since 1959, Léopold has been continuing their work in the second generation. He took over running it at the age of twenty-six years and has been doing so very successfully up until today with regular innovations. With his self-designed, unique steel column system made in France he creates a variety of rum style that are second to none.

Léopold Reimonenq tinkers around on each individual unit until he deems it perfect. Apart from the distillery, in 1989 he also opened the Musée du Rhum and in 1994 an enormous insect collection with 5,000 exhibits. In addition, a Guadeloupe exhibition and an impressive collection of model

101

*Distillery Reimonenq, Guadeloupe*

*Léopold Reimonenq*

shops. Whether the next generation, which is slow to take over, will continue all of this remains to be seen.

### J. R. on the rocks
🍶🍶🍶 / ▥▥ / 🪵 / 🥃

*Léopold's answer to the advice of his doctor to drink less. A lighter, "healthier" rum that should be drunk "on the rocks". Of course, even without ice it would work, since it is not light by far – but perfectly made. The initials stand for Joseph Reimonenq, his uncle and founder of the distillery, with whose oil painting he exchanges a couple of words every night before going to sleep.*

### Reimonenq 7 ans
🍶🍶🍶🍶 / ▥▥ / 🪵 / 🥃

*The flagship among Reimonenq's "vieux rhums". This is how a perfectly balanced rhum agricole from Guadeloupe tastes.*

## Distillerie Longueteau

For the local market, the rum is also bottled under the name Mon Repos, while for the international market the distillery uses the owner's name Longueteau. Distilling has taken place here since 1895 – when Henri Longueteau bought the sugar factory L'Esperance and converted it into the Longueteau distillery. In 1940 he also bought the little distillery Mon Repos, which he closed again in 1962. Even so, the name has lived on until today. Since 2006, François Longueteau has been running the business. There is neither electric light nor electric pumps for the mash in the distilling shed. Everything is still like in the "good old days". One of the few small family enterprises that only use their own sugarcane for their rhum agricole. The canne bleue and canne rouge types are cultivated and harvested just once a year. Here the basic product is still the focal point.

*Longueteau 6 ans*

🍾🍾🍾🍾 / ▨▨▨ / 🗡 / ⬚

*Slightly sweetish, easy to drink rhum agricole in the old style.*

# Distillerie Bologne

The white rhum agricole by Bologne is omnipresent on Guadeloupe. Those who drink a Ti' Punch here are mostly getting rum from this distillery.

Its history reaches back to 1654 when the De Bologne family arrived in Guadeloupe. This family history delivers a fine example of this time of colonialisation and the role of sugar.

Originating from the Dauphiné region in France, they emigrated to the Netherlands in the 16th century. Some family members emigrated further to Brazil at the end of the century, where the Dutch had settled in the area around Recife. They successfully ran sugar plantations there until the Dutch troops lost the Battle of Guararapes in 1654 and the family had to flee. With a fleet of ships with 1,200 refugees on board, they reached Martinique the same year. Being Protestants, they were not allowed to moor there, as a royal decree had forbidden this. They continued to Guadeloupe. The governor there, Charles Houël, paid little heed to the decree and welcomed the refugees. As the Dutch had signed a capitulation agreement with the Portuguese, the family De Bologne had not lost their wealth. They used it to found the sugar plantation on the site where the Distillerie Bologne still stands today. In the years that followed, the sugar factory experienced various owners, went bankrupt several times and was auctioned off in 1887. Henri de Pombirau bought the estate, built a distillery, and started to distil rum. After his death, he bequeathed the property to his nephews and nieces, who sold it to Louis Sargenton-Callard in 1930. He was specialized in the production of white rhum agricole, with which the Callard family is successful up until today.

### *Bologne blanc "Black Cane"*
🍾🍾🍾 / ▣ / 🚬 / 🗄

*The "Black Cane" type of sugarcane is almost never planted anymore because of its small yield. However, as it has exceptional taste properties, it continues to be cultivated at Bologne. A limited quantity also makes it to the market as a pure white rhum agricole. Very nicely fruity and pleasant, for the perfect Ti' Punch.*

## Domaine de Séverin

This "domaine" received its name from a Mr. Séverin, who purchased the former sugar plantation Bellevue in the 18th century and then converted it into a pineapple jam factory. In the 1920s, Madame Beauvarlet took over the Domaine de Séverin. Her nephew Henri Marsolle was appointed to start production of rhum agricole. He purchased the estate from his aunt and later passed it on to his two sons Joseph and Eduard. Eduard died in 1964 whilst trying to rescue a worker from a steam boiler explosion. Joseph and his wife May are involved with this distillery up until today, but it is primarily run by their sons.

### *Séverin blanc*
🍾🍾🍾 / ▣ / 🚬 / 🗄

*Good and cleanly distilled rhum agricole.*

# Domaine de Courcelles

The Courcelles distillery closed its doors in 1964. Where it once stood, there are now a couple of houses and a warehouse. The distilling apparatus was brought to the distillery of Sainte-Marthe, which produced Rhum Courcelles for a further eight years until it also closed. The last rum from the distillery was stored in vats for over thirty-five years at the Distillerie Poisson on Marie-Galante.

The owner of Distillerie Poisson, Jean Brot, now uses the brand name again. However, for the "new" Courcelles, rum from his other distillery is used.

### *Rhumhouse Courcelles 1972*
🍾🍾🍾🍾 / ⬛⬛⬛⬛ / ♨ / 🏛

*This rum made from molasses is a witness to past times. It was created during the very last distillation on the old apparatus and stored over thirty-eight years in vats. Absolutely unique sweet molasses rum.*

# MARIE-GALANTE

In 1493 Columbus came to this little neighbouring island of Guadeloupe. One of his ships bore the name *Maria Galanda* and that is how the little island with a diameter of 15 kilometres got its name. It was – and is up until today – strewn with sugarcane fields and almost a hundred windmills that drive the sugar mills. Today the most important product of the island is no longer sugar, but rum. There are three producers to just 13,000 inhabitants. They are known for excellent quality.

## Distillerie Bielle

Rum was distilled here for the first time in 1900. After that the distillery saw various owners, until it was abandoned after the Second World War and fell into ruin. It was not until 1975 that Dominique Thiery took the reins and founded the Société d'Exploitation de la Distillerie Bielle with the community of heirs. The distillery was built up again under his direction and has worked its way up over the last forty years to become the top producer on Marie-Galante.

Here one can experience again today how rum has been produced for an eternity. Countless small-scale farmers bring their fresh and manually harvested sugarcane to the distillery on little carts twice a week. Often it is even an ox cart. It is virtually impossible to produce rum fresher and cleaner than here and the operators Dominique Thiery and his nephew Jérôme understand more than many others about how to handle vats. Although the greatest part of the production is white 59 % rum that is consumed directly on the island, the exceptional renown that the distillery has achieved comes from its "rhums vieux", which are mostly bottled in vat strength.

Since 2005, alongside the column still, two little German fruit brandy units stand here that belong to the multiple award-winning Italian fruit brandy and grappa distiller Vittorio Capovilla. Together with Bielle, he

*Mash tanks at Bielle, Marie-Galante*

111

produces a rum of a "European" kind here that expresses itself in a longer, cooler and closed fermentation, as well as in "cleaner" distilling processes, which is possible in these pot stills with additional distilling trays.

### Bielle blanc
🍶🍶🍶🍶 / ▣▣ / 🚬 / 📱

*Intensive, full-bodied white rum with a lovely sugarcane aroma.*

### Bielle brut de fût 2003
🍶🍶🍶🍶 / ▣▣ / 🚬 / 📱

*A truly great rum, in which the vat comes perfectly to the fore. Rich in content. Unique, accomplished, and very limited.*

### Bielle brut de fût 2010
🍶🍶🍶🍶 / ▣▣ / 🚬 / 📱

*This "millésime" is also very accomplished. A hint fruitier, but also extremely rich in content and impressive.*

### Liberation 2015
🍶🍶🍶 / ▣▣ / 🚬 / 🍶 & 📱

*Regarding the rum project that Bielle runs together with the grappa distiller Vittorio Capovilla, some things are different. The sugarcane juice is fermented longer and at lower temperatures than usual and is distilled in little German fruit brandy units. In fact, the Liberation is produced as if it were grappa – but in the Caribbean and not from pomace. It is stored for six years in vats.*
*It is still a typical Bielle rum, perhaps a little lighter, cleaner, and fruitier, but in any case very interesting.*

# Distillerie Poisson

The rum from this distillery is named after the Dominican priest Père Labat from Paris. He was sent to the island at the end of the 17th century to set up a hospital for the poor and brought modern equipment for producing pure alcohol. Soon it was also used for rum production – a turning point for the French islands, as one now had a high level of technical knowledge and was able to achieve better production efficiency. Still today, many rum production traditions can be traced back to "Father" Labat.

The story started in 1860 when Catherine Poisson founded the sugar factory named after her. The distillery was not created until 1916, under the new owner Edouard Rameaux who had acquired the property in 1900. It was also he who was to give the rum the name of the famous priest later. In the beginning, distilling was still on a little pot still from Barbados and after 1955, on a column still that is still in operation today. From 1976 his nephew Ernest Renault led the company. He is an uncle of Dominique Thiery who revitalized the Distillerie Bielle at almost the same time. During the 1990s, the two distilleries even built a cellar together near the distillery to store their rums in vats. However, Poisson was less and less profitable and was finally sold in the year 2000. Under the new owners one can sense little innovation, however, so that at the moment there is only a white rum still on the market.

## Père Labat blanc

*The white rhum agricole is solid and is very well suited to the traditional Ti' Punch.*

## Père Labat 6 ans

*The six-year-old of Père Labat is unfortunately scarcely available anymore and is a very individual rhum agricole. A lot of sweetness and very distinctive fruit aromas make one almost think there was even a bit of molasses rum in the mix. In any case, it is very enjoyable to drink.*

*Metal column still, Guyana (Photo: Joshua Singh)*

# GUYANA

Guyana lies on the east coast of northern South America and in its history it has experienced various colonial powers. Present-day Guyana consisted in the 17$^{th}$ and 18$^{th}$ centuries of the originally Dutch colonies Essequibo, Demerara, and Berbice. These three colonies were assigned officially to Great Britain and Ireland at the Vienna Congress of 1815, from which the country did not gain independence until 1966. Rum from Guyana is still referred to today as Demerara rum. For a long time, the lion's share of British makes of rum came from Guyana, but of the former 200 distilleries now only a single one remains. In the 18$^{th}$ century, each plantation exported its own rum and labelled it with a mark. What was special about this was that the large distilleries used completely different distilling techniques, resulting in very varying rum styles. There were single and double columns made of metal or wood, as well as single and double pot and vat stills. For the wooden distilling units, which had to withstand very hot temperatures, extremely hard tropical woods were used, so-called ironwood.

## Demerara Distillers Ltd.

In the year 1983 the Uitvlugt, Enmore, and Diamond distilleries merged to become the company Demerara Distillers. The various vat, Coffey, and column stills from the distilleries were then brought to Demerara Distillers and still stand there today. The distillery is therefore a kind of live rum museum, where these ancient facilities are still in operation and produce large quantities of rum. The last wooden Coffey (column) still remaining in use worldwide stands there, as well as a single- and a double-vat still. These are actually pot stills whose lower part where the molasses is heated is built like a wooden cask. In addition, there are a fourfold column unit and a metal Coffey still. With all this equipment, the distillery is one of the largest producers of bulk rum in terms of volume, as well as the most various. This rum is sold open and therefore finds its way into a wide variety of blends around the world.

In our part of the world, one can primarily find their flagship, the El Dorado rum. However, the various styles are occasionally still available through independent bottlers who buy vats from the individual stills.

A little overview of the stills that are currently in use at Demerara Distillers and the names and marks:

**Double wooden "vat still":**
    *Sugar estate: Port Mourant*
    *Distillery: Albion, then Uitvlugt, then Diamond*
    *Marks: PM, AW, MPM*

**Single wooden "vat still":**
    *Sugar estate: Versailles & Lusignan*
    *Distillery: Versailles, then Enmore, then Uitvlugt, then Diamond*
    *Marks: VSG, KFM, SXG*

**Wooden "Coffey still":**
    *Original sugar estate: Enmore*
    *Distillery: Enmore*
    *Marks: EHP, ELCR, MD*

**Metal fourfold column "Savalle still":**
    *Sugar estate: Uitvlugt*
    *Distillery: Uitvlugt*
    *Marks: ICBU, AN, LBI, B, SWR, GS*

**Metal "Coffey still":**
    *Sugar estate: Diamond*
    *Distillery: Diamond*
    *Marks: SVW, SV*

*The wooden Enmore still, Guyana (Photo: DDL)*

*Port Mourant still, Guyana (Photo: DDL)*

## *El Dorado 12 yo*
🍾🍾🍾🍾 / 🧊🧊🧊🧊 / ♨ / ⚗🏺 & 🏢

*This rum is sweetish, but still heavy with parts from both distilling systems: EHP and **SVW** (in bold = more dominant proportion).*

## *El Dorado 15 yo*
🍾🍾🍾 / 🧊🧊🧊🧊 / ♨ / ⚗🏺 & 🏢

*This is a sweet and very rich rum with contents from four different distilling systems: EHP, **PM**, VSG, SVW.*
*This results in a perfectly balanced rum that is often considered a reference for mature heavy rum.*

## *El Dorado 21 yo*
🍾🍾🍾 / 🧊🧊🧊🧊 / ♨ / ⚗🏺 & 🏢

*A little sweeter still and fuller, with parts from three distilling systems: EHP, VSG, **AN.***

## Uitvlugt Distillery

The Uitvlugt Distillery (pronounced: "eyeflat") was located to the west of Georgetown and was permanently shut down in the year 2000. Originally a French Savalle still was used at this distillery, as mentioned above. However, Uitvlugt also had a double-vat still from Port Mourant and a single-vat still from Versailles, until they went to the Diamond Distillery after closure, the site of Demerara Distillers Ldt.

## *Uitvlugt 14 yo Cadenhead's*
🍾🍾🍾🍾🍾 / 🧊 / ♨ / ⚗

*This rum from the independent bottler Cadenhead's is labelled with the mark PM. This means that it comes from the Port Mourant still, which stood at Uitvlugt at* the time. It is bottled at vat strength, which in this case means 70.7% and is rather a proud value for a rum with fourteen-year storage.

Slight diluting with water is recommended to bring out the many aromas. Extremely heavy, full aroma, "dirty" rum in a British style.

## Enmore Distillery

The original Enmore style is medium-heavy and came from a wooden Coffey still (column still). The apparatus is more or less identical with the first column unit that the Irishman Aeneas Coffey invented in 1832. When the Versailles Distillery was closed in 1966 after the independence of Guyana, its famous single-vat still also came to Enmore. These two legendary stills went to Demerara Distillers in 1995.

### Enmore Distillery 11yo W. D. J. Marketing

W. D. J. Marketing was an independent bottler that does not exist anymore. This is therefore a rum from a closed distillery and a closed bottler. The label does not have a mark, so it is all rather vague. Instead of a mark, however, it says: "pot still". It must therefore have been a rum that comes from a Versailles vat still and it could have been distilled before 1995 and therefore at the original site. This rum has extreme wood aromas that are almost reminiscent of the cork aroma of a wine. Otherwise heavy, complex and rather unique in its kind.

### Enmore 1990 25yo Cave Guildive

From the legendary "Versailles still" when it still stood at the Enmore Distillery. A rum with great elegance that contains everything that has made this vat still so famous. Despite twenty-five years in the cask, still youthfully fresh and at the same time one can sense the concentrated complexity that such long storage brings with it. An absolutely great rum.

# Port Mourant Distillery

The Port Mourant Distillery was founded sometime in the early 19th century and closed between 1954 and 1958 – probably in the year 1955, but it cannot be precisely verified. Their distilling apparatus was a double wood pot still, so actually a vat still. This has a very particular, unmistakable aroma profile and produces some of the heaviest and most interesting rums in the world. After closure, the still was taken to the Albion distillery and continued to run there until its end – sometime between 1966 and 1969. After that it was taken to Uitvlugt Distillery and finally to Demerara Distillers, where it still stands and produces today.

## Port Mourant 1974 Velier

*An ancient bottling by Velier. Not many of these bottles exist worldwide anymore and they are very sought-after.*
*Unique, extremely concentrated variety of aromas with a strong wood incidence.*

## Port Mourant 2005 10 yo Cave Guildive

*A relatively young bottling of a classical Port Mourant, which is therefore still rather coarse and wild. Rum must have tasted somewhat like this 200 years ago.*

# FRENCH-GUYANA

As French-Guyana has had the status of a French overseas territory since 1946, rhum agricole may also be produced here officially. Sugar and rum do not play a major economic role. Today the European space travel station located here has the greatest importance. The area was discovered back in 1498 by Columbus. The first Europeans who settled here were the Dutch – followed in the 17th century by the French and British. The nation became very well-known especially due to its penal colony on the Îles du Salut in front of it, which existed from 1852 to 1951. One of the 70,000 inmates was Henri Charrière, who succeeded in escaping to British-Guyana in 1944. He reflected on his experiences in the book *Papillon* that was published in 1970 and was a worldwide success.

## Rhum Saint Maurice

In the village with the wonderful name Saint-Laurent-du-Maroni stands the only "rhumerie" of French-Guyana. The sugar factory and the distillery were founded in the first half of the 20th century and were extensively renovated in 2012. Multiple award-winning rhums agricoles are produced here on a big column still, with hand-cut local sugarcane.

### *La Belle Cabrese*

**â â â / ▨ / ◗ / ▥**

*Classical white rhum agricole which is usually enjoyed locally as Ti' Punch. It is very suitable for this with its pleasant sugarcane aroma.*

## Toucan No. 4

*Toucan is a professionally cultivated brand that works with rum from Saint Maurice. Apart from the white, the founder Catherine Arnold and her husband also like experimenting with wood. Toucan no. 4 was cultivated in an Armagnac cask and "infused" with wood chippings. A very successful experiment, if a little too "woody" for my personal taste.*

# BRAZIL

Brazil is very important for rum production today. Brazil is by far the largest sugarcane producer in the world and many Caribbean producers source molasses from this country.

No doubt everybody knows caipirinha: the drink stormed the bars in Europe some years ago in such a way that it can almost no longer be ordered impartially. Caipirinha is in fact the Brazilian version of the Cuban daiquiri or the French Ti' Punch: sugar, lime, rum. The rum is called cachaça in Brazil and, like rhum agricole, it is distilled out of sugarcane juice. However, to reduce cachaça to just this one cocktail does not do justice to its long past.

With the Tratado de Tordesillas of 1494, Brazil was allocated to the Portuguese, who in turn handed over the Canary Islands, amongst others, to Spain. Perhaps this is how they had got to know the Canarian version of the sugarcane spirit, which had been introduced from Indonesia via Genoa, and had taken the idea with them across the Atlantic. Brazilian cachaça was allegedly already distilled around 1500. According to the Italian rum historian Marco Pierini, much is merely speculation – he had not yet been able to find proof that the Brazilian rum version is the oldest in the Americas. It is unclear, for example, whether the word cachaça indeed referred to the spirit, or rather the foam that results from heating the sugarcane juice. For Pierini, it is only definite that the earliest commercial rum production emerged in 1640 in Dutch Brazil, which would make the Brazilian rum older than that from Barbados, where the first written documentation of a rum sale is dated to 1703.

## Agroecològica Marumbi

Cachaça has been produced in Morrettes, at the foot of the Pico do Marumbi, since 1700. It is an organic "artisanal cachaça" that is produced here. This means that the sugarcane is harvested by hand and the cachaça is distilled in copper pot stills.

### Cask Adventures No. 3

🍶🍶🍶 / ⬛⬛⬛ / 🪵 / ⚗️

*For this bottling, a used bourbon cask in which a rhum agricole by Reimonenq from Guadeloupe was stored for five years was filled with cachaça. It has taken on plenty of sweetness and aromas of rhum agricole. A very interesting cachaça that can be drunk pure and makes cocktails full of character.*

# PERU

The national alcoholic drink in Peru, as in the neighbouring country Chile, is the brandy Pisco. Sugar is also cultivated in the Andes valleys and so molasses was also available. Even so, the country has no high standing in the world of rum. Switzerland is a very important economic partner of Peru, as 11 percent of all Peruvian exports come to our country. This is largely gold. It makes sense that the most well-known rum from Peru also in this country is called Millionario.

## Ron Millonario Distillery

The Millonario distillery in the north of Peru belongs to the Italian company Rossi & Rossi Srl., which contributes to shaping the market with the "Rum Nation" line. The distillery owns three old Scottish column stills and cultivates its rums in four Solera rows. The casks are made of American and Slavonian oak, the molasses come exclusively from Peru.

### *Ron Millonario 15 años*

*A good, very sweet and full rum, which is typical of the Latin-American style.*

## Destilerías Unidas S.A.C.

The largest distillery in the country was founded in 1929. It produces a variety of alcohol but is known internationally especially for its stored rums. In 2004, on its 75-year anniversary, it was completely renovated and modernized.

### *Cartavio 12 años Solera*

*This rum was launched for the 75th anniversary of the distillery. It was produced with the Spanish Solera system and then matured for at least twelve years in casks made of Slovenian oak.*

# COLOMBIA

The name of this country in the north of South America is derived directly from the name Christopher Columbus. When we think of Colombian exports, it is the famous coffee and notorious drug cartels that first come to mind. However, sugarcane and sugar are also important export items and it is not a big step from these to rum. The big world brands may not be at home here, but instead for example a variety of aniseed that is consumed generously by the local population.

## Industria Licorera de Caldas

The enterprise was founded at the beginning of the 20th century. Apart from the successful Aguardiente Cristal, the Ron Viejo de Caldas is also distilled here. In autumn 2011 the halls where the three-year-old rum was stored burnt down.

### Aguardiente Cristal

*Although it can no longer really be tasted, the starting point is rum. A borderline case in this book: half rum, half liqueur – and it smells like Sambuca. This is actually not so unusual, because it is quite simply a flavoured rum that is made by many renowned producers (e.g. Malibu, Captain Morgan). In this case, it is the aniseed that gives it flavour. Little rum, a lot of aniseed. Recommended chilled.*

### Viejo de Caldas 3 años

*The classic from Colombia, which can often be scarce due to the fire in 2011. Nothing special, but typical of a very simple, young Latin-American rum.*

# VENEZUELA

Venezuela plays a major role in rum production, because many Caribbean distilleries currently resort to Venezuelan molasses as their local sugar industry has become too small. However, local products also do themselves proud. As one of the few South American countries, pot stills are also used in Venezuela alongside the customary column stills.

## Destilerías Unidas S. A.

Destilerías Unidas is a Venezuelan conglomerate of various manufacturers. It was founded in 1959 by Seagram's and for a time the company also belonged to Diageo. It produces cacique rum and various other spirits.

### Diplomático Reserva Exclusiva

🍾🍾🍾 / ▨▨▨▨▨ / 🥄 / ⚗ & 🛢

*This rum has experienced an incredible success story in recent years. However, this is unfortunately also because a lot of sugar is added. The more sugar that is added retrospectively to the alcohol, the "easier" it is to drink. We are all familiar with this from liqueurs. The actual distilled product, however, becomes rather secondary.*

*A pot still at Diplomatico, Venezuela (Photo: DU)*

*The cooper at work, Venezuela (Photo: DU)*

# PANAMA

Although sugarcane from Panama has a certain importance, it rarely reaches our part of the world in the form of rum. This is no doubt also due to the fact that, economically speaking, everything there stands in the shadow of the famous Canal. Furthermore, there is only one single commercial rum distillery – Varela Hermanos S. A. The Panama style is a little reminiscent of the Cuban, except that the rum has a little more "weight". The most famous master blender in the country used to work at Havana Club: Francisco "Don Pancho" Fernandez.

## Varela Hermanos S. A.

The roots of this distillery go back to the year 1908. Today it is a very large producer that manufactures a variety of alcohol. However, it is still in family hands. They use only their own sugarcane that is still cut by hand. Apart from their own brands, Ron Abuelo and Ron Cortez, large volumes of white and stored rum are sold to a range of bottlers and processors. Bacardi also distilled here for a long time. Zafra, Malecon or Ron de Jeremy, for example, come from this distillery, as well as the rum Maja from El Salvador.

The bottlers are countless, including all the important ones such as Nation, Cadenhead's, Duncan Taylor, A. D. Rattray, Berry Bros & Rudd, Plantation, and Samaroli.

### Ron Abuelo 7 años
🍼🍼🍼 / 🎲🎲🎲🎲 / 💩 / 📖

*The Abuelo 7 años is the classic from this distillery. A sweet rum with a good balance.*

### Panama 11yo 2006 Cave Guildive
🍼🍼🍼🍼 / 🎲🎲🎲 / 💩 / 📖

*There is little bottling from Panama in cask strength. Although the rum is a 60%
single cask bottling, it almost feels rather "mild". Apart from the traditional nutty
hints, there are also strong fruity aromas. A very exciting and somewhat untypical
Panama rum.*

# COSTA RICA

This little country between Panama and Nicaragua is often called the "Switzerland of Central America". It abolished its army in 1983, declared "active permanent and unarmed neutrality" and has been largely spared from social unrest and civil war in its history – quite untypical for the region.

Columbus landed here in 1502, and from 1560 the country was systematically colonized. However, as it has a strategically uninteresting location and is poor in natural resources, Costa Rica always remained an underdeveloped colony that was able to achieve independence as early as 1821.

Sugar and therefore also rum do not play such a significant role here as in many other countries. The main export goods are bananas, followed by pineapple and coffee.

## Centenario Internacional S.A.

In 1969, the major corporation Seagram's founded a subsidiary in Costa Rica that has been called Cisa since 2002 and has belonged to the Wisa Group from Panama since 2003. The distillery works with sugarcane from Costa Rica and uses large column stills. The maturation takes place in oak casks and in the Solera system.

### *Centenario 20 años*

🍾🍾 / 🎲🎲🎲🎲🎲 / 🧂 / 📑

*Nicely accomplished, sweet and full-bodied. A typical Latin-American rum with the addition of a lot of sugar.*

# NICARAGUA

Rum has been commercially produced in Nicaragua since 1890. It is usual for the local rums to have long maturation times, even the white rums remain in the cask for a few years. The most well-known and multiple award-winning rum from this country is Flor de Caña. The storage is untypical of Latin America: while the Solera system is used almost everywhere, the rum is stored here in small oak casks for as long as is indicated on the bottle.

## Compañia Licorera de Nicaragua

The distillery belongs to Grupo Pellas. The conglomerate of around fifty different companies includes banks, telecommunications and food companies. However, the core business has always been sugar. In the 1960s, the sugar plantation in Chichigalpa was the most productive producer in Central America. Then the Sandinista government under Daniel Ortega nationalized the factory of the oligarchs and the owner family Pellas went back and forth between the U.S.A. and Nicaragua during the Central America War. After the peace process of 1987, the family started to build up its fortune again – with success, as the present-day owner of the company, Carlos Pellas, became the first and hitherto only billionaire in the country. The Compañia offers various rums that differ especially in maturation time, between four and twenty-five years. The casks are stored still today in the original building, without air conditioning, temperature regulators or humidifiers. This so-called "slow-aged" procedure is considered essential here for allowing the rum to mature undisturbed. The reputation of the traditional company is frequently overshadowed by calls for boycott. Many former plantation workers suffer from chronic kidney failure or have already died of it. In Chichigalpa, this cause of death is six times more frequent than the average in Nicaragua. Almost half of all men in the village die of it. This could be due not only to the highly intensive use of pesticides, but also to the fact that the contract workers are paid according to the harvested quantity. They therefore take too few breaks and drink too little, which worsens the kidney problems. The company has so far denied all claims.

### *Flor de Caña 7 años*

**ii** / 🧊🧊🧊 / 💩 / 🍾

*Even the seven-year-old shows very well how the company works. Not as sweetened as many other Latin American rums.*

### *Flor de Caña 12 años*

**ii** / 🧊🧊🧊 / 💩 / 🍾

*The same applies to the twelve-year-old. A good, balanced rum without too much of a wood emphasis, despite long storage.*

### *Nicaragua 2004 13yo Cave Guildive*

**iii** / 🧊🧊 / 💩 / 🍾

*A single cask bottling by the Zurich bottler Guildive. This is how Nicaraguan rum tastes without the addition of caramel or sugar. Rounded, full-bodied, a little smoky and with a light sweetness.*

*The column for Flor de Caña is housed here, Nicaragua*

# GUATEMALA

During the colonial era, Guatemala distinguished itself especially as a coffee producer. Rum was already made back then, but the first commercial distillery was not established until 1914. Today it is especially the Zacapa that enjoys world renown and wins international prizes.

All Guatemalan rums come from the same distillery and are distilled from "virgin sugarcane honey". This term is translated directly from the Spanish (*miel de caña*) and did not exist in English before that. This light form of molasses, both in terms of weight and colour, is simply called "first molasses" or "light molasses". The juice from sugarcane is heated so that the amount of water is reduced and the proportion of sugar is at least 72 percent. For the fermentation, however, the juice must be diluted with water again, as otherwise the yeast dies off. Through heating, the sugarcane syrup is made durable.

## Licorera Zacapaneca

The producer of Zacapa rum is Licorera Zacapaneca, which belongs to Industrias Licoreras de Guatemala that also produces the Botran rums. The brand Zacapa belongs in turn to the multinational spirits corporation Diageo.

Neither molasses nor sugarcane juice are used here, but instead "virgin sugarcane honey", which basically means pasteurized sugarcane juice. The maturation takes place at an altitude of 2,332 metres in a so-called double Solera, as is used for sherry.

## Zacapa 23 Solera

A cut from different casks that rum was stored in for between three and twenty-three years. This rum contributed significantly to the present-day popularity of this spirit. As it is considerably sweetened, it does appeal to the wide masses. The style of Zacapa is copied today by many other producers. However, unfortunately the quality has not necessarily improved along with its great success.

*Firing with pressed sugarcane (Photo: Carlos R. Cervantes)*

# MEXICO

Of course, Mexico stands primarily for its agave spirits – tequila, mezcal and their relatives are omnipresent. With its long east coast, Mexico also has Caribbean influence though – and good rum is also distilled. Of the many distilleries that have emerged in recent years, however, none have yet achieved a big breakthrough.

## Licores Veracruz

This family-run enterprise on the coast of the Gulf of Mexico produces a variety of spirits. For over sixty years, the Villanueva family has been producing tequila, mezcal, liqueurs, vodka, and the rums Mocambo and Los Valientes on pot and column stills – but for a long time only for the Mexican market. Some spirits have been exported in recent years.

### Los Valientes 10 años

*This rum has a rather unique composition. It is made from molasses (30 percent) and sugarcane juice (70 percent), which gives it an interesting flavour spectrum. The grassy, fresh notes from the juice and the sweet, heavy notes from the molasses readily come to the fore. The sugarcane juice distillate is distilled in pot stills, the molasses distillate in column stills.*

## Trapiche José Luis

In the mountains of the federal state Oaxaca, amidst the homeland of mezcal, José Luis Carrera is the third generation to distil rum – or as he would call it, aguardiente de caña. On 14 hectares he cultivates four different types of sugarcane alongside coffee and fruit. Distilling takes place in a copper column still with six trays.

## Paranubes 54 %

*The juice of the freshly squeezed local sugarcane is fermented – like mezcal – in large, open casks made of pine wood. José Luis removes only half of the fermented mash after forty-eight hours and fills the cask again with fresh sugarcane juice. He thus keeps the fermentation going continuously over four months. To restart the fermentation, he adds the boiled bark of the mesquite tree to the cask instead of yeast. Fermentation therefore takes place here completely without water and yeast.*

*The rum smells of fresh sugarcane and is reminiscent of the Clairins from Haiti. On the palate, however, it is somewhat coarser and a little fizzy even. A very authentic, unadorned rum that does not conceal its simple production.*

*José Luis Carrera at the mash vat (Photo: Carlos R. Cervantes)*

*Oaxaca, Mexico (Photo: Carlos R. Cervantes)*

# MADAGASCAR

Madagascar is the fourth-largest island in the world and is sometimes also called the "eighth continent". The flora and fauna have been able to develop completely independently owing to the geographical isolation over millions of years. The island lies in front of the east coast of Mozambique in the Indian Ocean. Apart from vanilla, cloves, and other spices, sugar is an important agricultural product. 40,000 tons of it are produced every year.

## Compagnie Vidzar

The distillery was founded in 1982 in Dzamandzar. It is on the little island Nosy Be, which is just a few kilometres in front of the northwest coast of Madagascar. In the year 1996, the founder of the company, Lucien Fohine, died. His son Franck took over the business and is still running it very successfully today. When he took the helm of the company he was only seventeen years old.

After he had taken over, Vidzar also started to store rum. The results are very positive. The rums are relatively sweet and one can truly sense the spices that enrich the air in Madagascar.

### Vieux Rhum Dzama 1998 10 ans

🍾🍾🍾 / 🧊🧊🧊🧊 / 🥄 / 📋

*Amber-coloured rum that has been stored for at least ten years in French Limousin oak casks. A very individual, well-made, pleasantly sweet rum.*

# LA RÉUNION

Île de la Réunion is a French overseas territory and is therefore entitled to produce "authentic" rhum agricole. This may officially be called as such only if it has been produced on French soil. Rum has been produced on this island in the Indian Ocean since 1704. Already before this, however, slaves drank a fermented sugarcane drink called fangourin.

Rhum agricole is produced, but because the big rum producers are associated with the sugar industry, a lot of "rhum traditionnel" is also made from molasses. The two styles will appeal more to lovers of strict, spicy-aromatic rum.

## Rhumerie Rivière du Mât

At this distillery, which is one of the oldest on the island, molasses from the two major sugar factories is processed. It is the largest producer of rum and alcohol on the island and it also distils rhum agricole made from sugarcane juice.

### Rhum agricole vieux cuvée spéciale

*Five- to eight-year cask storage. Wild and spicy, but nevertheless elegant.*

### Rhum traditionnel Grande Réserve

*A strong molasses rum with plenty of spice and character.*

# Distillerie Isautier

The smallest of the distilleries on La Réunion was founded as early as 1845 by the brothers Charles and Louis Isautier. It is in family ownership up until today and also the only one that is not linked to a sugar factory. The rum is produced both out of molasses and sugarcane juice. Isautier brings out excellent qualities for both styles.

### Isautier Barrik

🥃🥃🥃 / 🧊🧊 / 🍯 / 🏭

*The youngest of the aged rums. It only spends three months in new French oak casks, but during this time it is infused with strong wood aromas, which are coupled pleasantly with the young, fruity, and wild style.*

### Isautier 7 ans

🥃🥃🥃 / 🧊🧊 / 🍯 / 🏭

*Apart from the Barrik, there is also three-year, five-year, and ten-year molasses rum. As is so often the case, the golden mean is the best: the seven-year-old brings together the fruit and wood aromas in the most perfect manner. A wonderful independent rum that unfortunately is often sold out.*

# Distillerie Savanna

The Rhumerie Savanna started operating in 1950. At this time, it was linked to the sugar factory of the same name, which ceased production in 1986. In 1992, the whole distillery was relocated to Saint-André, where one of the two remaining sugar factories on the island stands – the Usine de Bois Rouge. Now a lot of "open" rum is distilled here for other processors on several column stills. An old copper column still from the famous Parisian manufacturer Savalle is also still in operation here.

Even so, high-quality rum is produced here, which is brought onto the market under its own name. Both "rhum traditionnel" and "Grand Arôme" from molasses, as well as rhum agricole from sugarcane juice.

### Savanna 2003 Rhum agricole 11 ans

*Savanna has made a name for itself in recent years with single cask bottlings. A lot is tried out here – and not everything succeeds, but sometimes it is very good. For example, this rhum agricole that is matured in a cognac cask and at the end in a Calvados cask for the finish. Very accomplished, rounded, balanced, and interesting.*

*Trou d'Eau Douce, Mauritius*

# MAURITIUS

Mauritius lies in the Indian Ocean, 900 kilometres to the east of Madagascar and near the island of La Réunion and the island state of the Seychelles. Since 1969, the island group has been independent and a member of the Commonwealth. Before the British, power was held here by the Portuguese, Dutch, and French.

During the French era (1715–1810), the French East India Company that owned the island until 1767 had African slaves cultivate sugarcane plantations. Today more than 90 percent of the land surface is planted with sugarcane.

Despite this, until 2008 it was only permitted to manufacture "sugarcane spirit" with less than 37.5 % alcohol on Mauritius. It was not allowed to be called rum. Since then, the quality has gotten better every year and some new brands and distilleries have emerged.

At the same time, a lot of rum is produced that is then marketed by a variety of companies from around the world. There are various strongly sweetened or spiced rums from Mauritius that live mainly off clever marketing.

## Rhumerie de Chamarel

The Rhumerie de Chamarel is located in a national park and has existed since 2008. It exclusively produces rhum agricole on a little copper column still and a pot still. Four types of sugarcane are used that all grow on its own land.

The owner family comes from the luxury hotel business and runs the distillery almost like a resort. The guided tours are by "hostesses", a French top chef cooks at the restaurant; the meat comes from game living on their own land and is processed at their own butchery. The rhumerie therefore lives significantly from tourism and restaurant visitors. Nevertheless, very good rum is produced here with great care.

## Chamarel classic 52

🍶🍶🍶 / ▣▣ / 🍬 / 📖

*A very accomplished rhum agricole with a strong sugarcane taste. Perfectly suited to Ti' Punch.*

## Chamarel XO

🍶🍶🍶 / ▣▣ / 🍬 / 🏺 & 📖

*Two thirds of the XO come from the column still and one from the pot still. It is stored between six and eight years in three different types of cask.*

# Labourdonnais

The Domaine de Labourdonnais was established as early as 1774 – but the distillery was not started up until 2008. At first it bore the name Mascareignes and was run in partnership with Distillerie Isautier from the neighbouring island La Réunion. This partnership collapsed and the distillery took on the name of the sovereign domaine. It only processes its own sugarcane, which results in around 50,000 litres of rum per year, from sugarcane juice, which are distilled in a big, modern steel column still from South America.

## Labourdonnais blanc

🍶🍶🍶 / ▣▣ / 🍬 / 📖

*This white rum made from sugarcane juice has surprisingly few aromas of the sugarcane itself. The producer says that this is so because their sugarcane faces the strong ocean winds and is therefore a little more bitter. This is indeed possible, because the rum is clean and very interesting. Instead of the usual sweetness and fruitiness of the sugarcane, it is rather dry and a little "salty".*

*Small copper column at Chamarel, Mauritius*

*Large steel column at Grays, Mauritius*

# Rhumerie Saint Aubin

At Saint Aubin, the year 1819 is indicated on every bottle. It refers to the founding of the sugarcane plantation. The rhumerie, however, started with a little pot still by the Czech producer Hradecky Pacov that was put into operation in 2001. Ten years later, a column still with sixteen trays was added. It previously served a South African brandy manufacturer and can deliver significantly larger volumes of rum. Two quite differing rum styles are therefore distilled here. Some of it also goes into the "vanilla rum" to which some of their own vanilla is added. This speciality is very widespread in Mauritius, as excellent vanilla grows there.

### *Saint Aubin blanc agricole*

*The white rhum agricole from the pot still brings together a strong structure and pleasant fruit notes.*

# Grays Distilling Ltd.

This distillery is a typical example of the rather "unromantic" large-scale production of rum and alcohol, as often occurs in this business but is rarely shown. All kinds of things that can be distilled from molasses are produced in very large, efficient column stills. Apart from good rum, also spiced rum, liqueur, vodka and a lot of neutral alcohol. A large amount of it is shipped in large containers to the African continent, where it is processed further. The old sugar factory, whose machines were shut down in 1998 after 177 years of operation, was converted into a very informative and frequented museum on the topic of sugar production.

Today the molasses for the alcohol production comes from the Terra sugar factory. This belongs to a major investment group, along with the distillery newly developed in 1980.

The high-quality molasses is fermented for thirty-two hours and then distilled on an enormous column still. Until 2001, however, only neutral alcohol was produced here. For their own rum brand New Grove, the facilities were converted especially in 2003 so that the production of neutral alcohol and that of rum could be clearly separated. Storage takes place in casks of all sizes, half of which are new, unused casks made of Limousin oak, probably one of the strengths of Grays. Fairly average white rums become very good mature and balanced rums after storage.

### New Grove 8 yo
🝙🝙 / 🟦🟦 / 🝛 / 📖

*The eight-year-old from New Grove is for me an example of perfect work in the cellar. The wood is perfectly incorporated and the strong, distinct fruitiness, which only Limousin oak casks can bring forth, is unmistakable. A rum that is extremely good value for money.*

# PHILIPPINES

Christopher Columbus is attributed the honour of having brought sugarcane from the Canary Islands to the Caribbean region. However, the original homeland of the plant is East Asia and this giant grass has been indigenous in the Philippines since primeval times. In East Asia, it is mostly arrack (known as the "rum of the Asians") that is distilled from molasses, but in the Philippines there is a good selection of authentic rum, of which the Tanduay is the most well-known. The country is one of the largest rum producers and in terms of turnover the third-largest market in the world. The fact that the Spanish made colonial claims on the Philippines in 1565 also had an influence on the rum style. The Philippine rums are rather mild and sweet and therefore remotely comparable with the rums from Spanish-speaking Latin America.

## Tanduay Distillers Inc.

The origins of this company date back to the year 1854. Three Spanish merchants founded a trade enterprise that acquired the local steam ship company. Later on a distillery was added and today Tanduay is one of the largest rum distilleries in the world in terms of produced volume.

### Tanduay 12 yo

Simple, sweet rum with aromas of nut and caramel.

## Bleeding Heart Rum Company

On the island of Negros, sugarcane has been indigenous for centuries. The molasses used for the rum is supposed to come exclusively from the island. Distilling takes place at a large distillery in Manila. After that the rum matures for seven years back on Negros in casks made of American oak. This rum was launched by a Brit: Stephen Carroll previously worked in marketing at Diageo, Rémy Cointreau and LVMH – three of the most significant spirits manufacturers.

### *Don Papa*

*A pleasant dessert – with an incredible amount of sugar. Aromas of oranges, candied fruits, cinnamon, and vanilla. However, one cannot speak of any authentic rum taste here.*

*Nine Leaves owner Yoshiharu Takeuchi (Photo: Nine Leaves)*

# JAPAN

So far, very little is known in the west about Japanese rum production. In Europe, three types are currently available, one of which is distilled from sugarcane juice. The fact that Japan has a good knowledge of distillery has been proven by the great whisky tradition in the country. Furthermore, for a long time a so-called Shōchū has been distilled from molasses. It is worth trying the rums, in any case, as they have their very own style.

## Nine Leaves Distillery

The distillery, opened in 2013, lies on the island of Honshu, the largest of the Japanese archipelago. The founder, owner and master distiller Yoshiharu Takeuchi had had enough of his life as a car parts manufacturer at his father's company and decided to become a rum distiller. After three days of discussions with Ichiro Akuto, the owner of the Chichibu whisky distillery that had been started in 2008, he also decided to order little pot stills from Forsythe's in Scotland.

What is special in this case is the raw material. Takeuchi uses both loose sugar and sugar pressed into blocks from the island of Tarama, which is known for its sugarcane cultivation. He mixes the sugar with water, adds yeast and the mash is ready.

### Nine Leafes Clear
🍶🍶🍶 / 🧊🧊 / – / 🥃

*This unstored white rum is rather unusual, but very accomplished. Rather yeasty, but with pleasant hints of fruit.*

## Kikusui Shuzo Co Ltd

On the island of Shikoku, in Kuroshio, stands the Kikusui distillery. It belongs to the oldest sugarcane processor in Japan and is also known for its sake.

### *Ryoma 7 yo*

🍶🍶 / 🧊🧊 / 🍵 / 📖

*The Ryoma rum stored for seven years in an oak cask has a taste that is complex, slightly fruity, and fills the mouth. Very unusual and interesting.*

# NEPAL

What this country is known for are its Sherpas, Mount Everest, the Himalayas, but scarcely Nepalese rum. However, wherever the British have been they have left their traces and so rum is distilled at the Nepal Distilleries. Their rum is diluted to drinking strength with water from the Himalayas. In cold Nepal, the rum is often drunk with hot water or added to other warm drinks, but in a heated Central European bar it is recommended to enjoy it pure, as Khukri does not only distinguish itself by its bottle, but also by its taste.

## Nepal Distilleries Pvt. Ltd.

Nepal Distilleries was founded in 1959. It is based in Kathmandu, at the foot of the Himalaya. Earlier distilling was with a pot-still procedure, while today a continuous distilling facility is used. The flagship of the company is the Coronation Khukri.

### Coronation Khukri

What is noticeable at first is its unusual bottle. It has the form of a traditional Nepalese weapon and is handmade. The rum itself also presents itself as quite different from its Caribbean relatives. The special Himalaya wooden casks no doubt make their contribution – or perhaps it is the Himalayan water?
The special Coronation bottle was introduced in 1974 to mark the crowning of the new king: "Shree Panch Birendra Bir Bikram Shah Dev".

164

# INDIA

India is the most populous nation in the world after China. The local alcohol market is immense. Some of the largest whisky brands in the world are based here, names that one has hardly heard of here in this county. As the British had great influence for a long time, gin and rum enjoy a certain standing here, alongside whisky. In any case, more than enough of the main ingredient is available. After Brazil, India is the second-largest cultivation country for sugarcane.

## Mohan Meakin Ltd.

This company is situated in the state of Uttar Pradesh and still produces much more than just the Old Monk rum. It all started with beer. Today various whisky, brandy and gin brands have been added, alongside the already mentioned rum.

### Old Monk Gold Reserve 12 yo

*One of the most sold rums worldwide, as its local market is enormous – people in India enjoy their drink. A simple, sweet rum.*

## Amrut Distilleries

This famous whisky producer has been distilling since 1948 in Bangalore, the capital of the southern Indian state of Karnataka. Over 450 employees produce a variety of alcoholic drinks – including rum.

### Old Port Deluxe

*A rum without a stated age and a powerful sweetness from Indian molasses. Suitable with Cola or ginger beer.*

# INDONESIA

Indonesia is the largest archipelago state in the world, comprising 17,508 islands. In 1945 the nation declared independence from the former colonial power, the Netherlands, a declaration that was only accepted after a four-year war and under diplomatic pressure from the U.S.A. In return, the young republic had to take over enormous state debts.

Sugarcane has been indigenous here for millennia and still today, it is one of the most important agricultural products.

The capital Jakarta is on the island of Java that was called Batavia before the nation's independence. This is where the perhaps most direct ancestor of rum emerged centuries ago – arrack. Marco Polo first brought it to Europe in the 14$^{th}$ century, where it soon gained great popularity. Genoese merchants, who handled the arrack market as far as Russia, now put their money into sugar plantations on the European Mediterranean and Atlantic islands, where they produced a local sugarcane spirit that was supposed to replace the arrack imported at great cost from Asia.

On Java there is still arrack. It is still called Batavia Arrack and is subject to clear regulations. It is only distilled on Java – in pot stills and from molasses. The diluted molasses, however, also has little "cakes" of local red rice added. They serve the purpose of starting fermentation with their yeast spores.

Batavia Arrack is not to be mistaken for Ceylon Arrack, or the hundreds of other variants. Ceylon Arrack is distilled exclusively from fermented palm blossom wine and is therefore not rum.

## J. B. Labat Spirituosen

At the spirits shop J.B. Labat in Zurich, we regularly had requests for a real Batavia Arrack. As there is practically nothing good on the market, we were able to have our own blend made by an arrack trader.

### *E. D. Dekker's Batavia Arrack*

🍾🍾🍾🍾 / ▢▢ / ☕ / ⚗️

*A blend of three different arracks from the same distillery, which has been stored for a year in teak wood casks. This arrack is very well suited to livening up old punch recipes for which there is often a demand for Batavia Arrack. However, it can also be enjoyed pure – the condition is pure enjoyment of plenty of taste!*

*Beenleigh Distillery, Australia (Photo: zvg)*

# AUSTRALIA

Australia produces more than 30 million tons of sugarcane per year. This is a good reason to include a rum from Oceania in the product range. The Colonial Sugar Refining Company (CSR) was founded back in 1855 and set up sugar refineries in Australia, New Zealand, and the Fiji Islands. Between 1890 and 1901, CSR also opened distilleries in various parts of Australia. In early colonial times, rum also served in Australia to remunerate convicts for their work.

The market leader is Bundaberg rum, which covers 95 percent of consumption of dark rum in Australia. However, there are also other products of a high standing.

## Beenleigh Distillery

The oldest distillery in Australia produces rum under its own name, which is practically never available abroad. The great and unfortunately rarely available Inner Circle is especially interesting. Originally this rum was produced by CSR exclusively for their own directorate and some important customers. When the sugar company sold its distilleries, the rum also disappeared. Stuart Gilbert bought the brand Inner Circle in the year 2000 and reactivated the legendary rum, together with the former Beenleigh master distiller Malcolm Campbell. He soon won all major awards. In 2007 Gilbert sold Inner Circle again and founded his own brand – Holey Dollar.

### Inner Circle Red

🍾🍾🍾🍾 / 🗃️🗃️ / 🝑 / 🏺

*Pure pot-still rum in the old style. The aromas of Jamaican and Demerara rum come together wonderfully here. A great rum for little money.*

# FIJI

Rum is even produced in the midst of the South Pacific, near the Date Line. The conditions for this are very good. Sugarcane of a very good quality grows here, owing to the ideal climate and volcanic soil. Even so, the islands do not have a great rum history.

## South Pacific Distilleries Ltd.

This distillery was opened in 1980 on Lautoka, the third-largest town on the main island Viti Levu. The area is considered the centre of sugar production and so it stood to reason that the excellent molasses should be processed further into rum at their own distillery. They work with old pot stills and column stills here. The rum stands up to comparison.

### *Holey Dollar Silver*

*Stuart Gilbert founded the company in 2008 with the aim of producing a rum in the "old style" for the 200-year anniversary of the Rum Rebellion (a successful uprising against the government in 1808). He kept the production method of his successful project, the Australian Inner Circle rum: the sugarcane comes from the Fiji Islands, distilling is in pot stills and maturation is in little oak casks. Within a very short timeframe, Gilbert also won various prizes with this rum.*
*A strong rum that is reminiscent of Jamaican rum. Highly aromatic, and lasting.*

### *Cave Guildive Fiji 2001–2016*

*A pure pot-still rum. Highly aromatic and quite varied. This rum can easily hold its own against the big Jamaican and Demerara rums.*

# U. S. A.

The United States of America are primarily known today for whiskies. The early settlers, however, drank a lot of rum.

In the thirteen eastern colonies that broke with the British crown in 1776, rum production was one of the most important branches of the economy. Half of the consumed rum was produced locally.

In just six months of the year 1688, in Massachusetts alone almost 600,000 litres of molasses were imported. Half of it was distilled to rum. The capital Boston and the nearby Medford became the epicentre of the so-called Medford rum. In the year 1770, the thirteen North American colonies distilled around 19 million litres of rum.

The molasses was imported from the British colonies of the Caribbean. The powerful plantation owners there were so fixated on their extremely lucrative sugar business that they cultivated practically nothing else. Everything needed had to be imported, mostly from North America. Molasses, on the other hand, was available almost endlessly and was popular as an article of exchange – it was a lot cheaper than their own grain that at the time was processed more for food than alcohol.

In the French colonies, however, molasses was even cheaper. After the North Americans therefore purchased more from the French, the duped English planters from Barbados and Antigua complained in London. The motherland Great Britain issued very high customs duties on foreign molasses in 1733 (Molasses Act). Further tax laws followed this first one. The increasing dissatisfaction of the northern colonies led decades later to the American War of Independence. Towards the end of the 18$^{th}$ century, American rum increasingly lost significance. Whisky was on the advance and rum was increasingly considered totally unmodern. In the year 1888, the number of rum distilleries in Boston had shrunk to three. The prohibition of 1917 finally eliminated the remainders of the American rum tradition.

The strong U. S. trend towards local products in recent years (and therefore also distilleries) has also affected the rum distilleries. There is still no distinct American style, but the scene is vibrant.

## GrandTen Distilling

This distillery started operating in the year 2012 and produces various other distillates alongside rum. As it is based in Boston, of course a rum also had to be included in its portfolio.

### *GrandTen Medford Rum*

🍶🍶🍶 / 🎲🎲🎲 / 🥄 / 🏭

*This rum is intended to revitalize the old Medford style. To what extent that has succeeded is difficult to say, as only few living people drank the "authentic" Medford rum. However, it is meant to be medium-heavy, rustic, and with a molasses emphasis. This can, by all means, be claimed of the GrandTen. It is distilled in little pot stills with blackstrap molasses, which is considered especially aromatic.*

## St. George Spirits

In California, the former Spanish and then Mexican colony, rum does not have a big tradition. This distillery is therefore known more for its gins in our part of the world. Alongside this, it produces various fruit brandies. It is hardly surprising, because it was the son of a German distiller from the Black Forest who founded the distillery in Oakland in 1982.

## California Agricole Rum
🍶🍶🍶🍶 / ▨ / ⬧ / ⚗

*This rum was born from the enjoyment of experimenting. In fact, nobody needs an expensive white rhum agricole from California. The people from St. George know that, too. However, as wonderful sugarcane grows in southern California, this is nevertheless a good enough reason for them. The rum is fun – for those who like strong aromas.*

# SPAIN

Spain is not really famous for rum, although it practically all started here: after all, Columbus took the sugarcane from the Canary Islands to the West Indies. The Spanish influence on rum history is therefore immense, even if few sugarcane fields remain in the country on the southern Costa Tropical. The fields that formerly stretched from Valencia to Gibraltar were ever less profitable than the lure of the real estate industry. However, rum is still distilled in Spain and Bacardi has a factory here for the European market.

The Spanish style is mild and natural, with maturation in so-called bodegas and in the Solera system.

## Ron Montero S. L.

The Bodega Montero has existed since 1963. Francisco Montero Martin first produced vodka and then gin. In the end he decided on rum after all, the traditional drink from the area of Motril, where the bodega and distillery stand. A few years ago, the enterprise was supposed to be sold. There were plenty of interested parties, including Bacardi. Despite this, the company remained in family hands and the next generation took over. The alcohol is distilled on a continuous distilling unit and is then taken to the bodega, where it matures in new 500-litre casks made of American oak – in the traditional Solera system, as is also used for sherry. It wanders for years from cask to cask and is then bottled. In the area it is often drunk as "Palito de Ron" – with lemonade added in a big glass.

### Ron Montero Gran Reserva

*At least four years in the cask. Mild and rounded, but with a strong hint of wood.*

## Destilerías Aldea S. L.

This Canarian distillery was built in 1936 on the west coast of Gran Canaria. The owner Don Manual Quevedo Alemán had learned his trade on Madeira, then the European hub of rum production. Gran Canaria also offered ideal soil for cultivating sugarcane. However, at the end of the 1950s the local farmers focused on the more productive tomato and the distillery was forced to close in 1959. Ten years later, two of Alemán's sons restarted production on the neighbouring island La Palma.

### *Ron Aldea Familia*

*Aldea distils rum from sugarcane juice and not molasses – in February during the sugarcane harvest the factory runs at full pelt. Relatively mild, with a pleasant sweetness and very harmonious.*

*Companhia des Engenhos do Norte, Madeira (Photo: Mario Thomas)*

# PORTUGAL

Like Spain, Portugal has a great significance in the history of rum. The Portuguese contributed significantly to the worldwide spread of the drink. After arrack had found its way to Europe with Marco Polo, the Portuguese were among the first who attempted to produce it themselves. In 1490 they were even the largest sugar producer in the world. With the islands São Tomé and Príncipe, which they colonized at the end of the 14th century, and Madeira, which had been in Portuguese hands since 1419, they had the perfect conditions for successful sugarcane cultivation. Rum is produced up until today on both island groups.

In Madeira they already mastered the necessary techniques in the 15th century. The first sugarcane plants were sent to the island in 1425 from Sicily by Henry the Navigator and the success of the sugar industry was enormous. Various churches and palaces were built with the profit and as Madeira was an important stop on the way to the "New World", the plants and the knowledge were carried on to many other countries. However, as early as the 18th century this led to the slow decline of local sugar production. Other Atlantic islands and the colonies of the "New World" were even more successful, whereupon Madeira focused more on wine cultivation.

At a time when Columbus was setting out to America, a drink was already being consumed here that was attributed later to the Caribbean. The way there led via Brazil, which was assigned to Portugal in 1494 and is one of the largest sugar producers up until today. Just like on Madeira, the rum is distilled directly from the fermented sugarcane juice – in Brazil as cachaça and in Madeira as aguardente de caña.

## Companhia des Engenhos do Norte Lda

This factory stands on the little town of Porto da Cruz, which evokes the glorious era of sugar production on Madeira. It was built in 1927, but some of the machines date back to the 18<sup>th</sup> century. An old steam machine provides heating and distilling is performed in copper column stills. A little alambic charentais is also still in operation here, but only for small productions.

### *Branca*

*This rum is somewhere between rhum agricole and cachaça. Nice, strong sugarcane taste.*

### *Aguardente de Cana 970 Reserva*

*The Reserva is stored for six years in casks made of French oak. It has a distinctive wood taste and is very dry. Very individual and interesting.*

## Engenho Novo da Madeira

The origins of this enterprise go back to the year 1845 when Harry Hinton founded the Fábrica do Torreão and started to distil rum from sugarcane juice. His father William was an English businessman who came to the island in 1838 and earned his money with bananas, among other things. Hinton's rum soon earn a good reputation and the distillery produced until 1986. After that it was demolished – the Santa Luzia park now stands in its place. The big chimney is integrated into the park and is supposed to recall the legendary era of the sugar industry.

*Madeira (Photo: Jonas Schwarz)*

As demand increased again, at the beginning of the century the farmers started cultivating more sugarcane again. And an heir of the Hinton family decided to distil rum again and founded the Engenho Novo in 2006. They distil using the original old (restored) copper column still of the Fábrica do Torreão.

### William Hinton Ediçào Limitado
🍼🍼🍼 / ▨ / 🪵 / 🏭

*A limited white 69 % rum made of sugarcane juice that has run through natural fermentation. A very interesting rum that is wonderfully fruity, very dry, and a little salty.*

### William Hinton Madeira Cask
🍼🍼🍼 / ▨ / 🪵 / 🏭

*William Hinton has a whole range of stored rums that have been matured in a variety of casks. The Madeira cask is rather interesting. It nicely combines the sweetness of Madeira wine with the dry style that used wine casks bring with them. In addition, there is the saltiness of this rum. Very complex.*

*Distillery Calheta, Madeira (Photo: Jonas Schwarz)*

# SWITZERLAND

Rum is also distilled in Switzerland, even if it is rather rare. As the starting product must always be sugarcane, molasses is imported – sugar beet grows in Switzerland, but it is mostly processed to ethanol. However, in recent times even the beets are increasingly processed into "rum-like" spirits, but by law it may not be called rum.

## Brennerei Humbel

Together with the "Kirsch" distiller Lorenz Humbel, I visited the organically producing sugar factory Baliño in Cuba in 2010. The Humbel distillery in Aargau distils a rum in a Cuban style from their organic molasses. As is usual in Cuba, it is filtered through activated charcoal.

### Guajira blanco

*A cleanly distilled white rum with a sweetish taste made of organic molasses. Perfect for classical Cuban cocktails.*

### Cask Adventures No. 5

*Marc Rohner, blender from Brennerei Humbel, and I undertook experiments with the Guajira rum and other spirits with various cask storages. These are each very limited bottlings. For the Cask Adventures No. 5, white distilled Guajira rum was stored for a good two years in a large cognac cask and then for a few months in a used Mezcal cask. A light, clean, but nevertheless complex rum.*

## Brennerei Erismann

Hans Erismann belongs to the fourth generation that distils fruit brandies and many other things in Bülach. Apart from its multiple award-winning raspberry brandy, the gin that is obligatory nowadays, and a whisky, since 2017 it also has its own rum.

### *Ron Juan Züri Rum*

*Clean distilled white rum, with pleasant sweetness. Stored for a short period in oak casks for harmonization.*

*Vat cellar at Humbel, Switzerland*

*Humbel distillery, Switzerland*

*Sugarcane harvest, Guyana (Photo: DDL)*

# COCKTAILS

## Punch

The British had brought the recipe for the rum punch from India to the new colonies in the Caribbean. The Hindi word for "five" is "panch" and indicates the number of ingredients that were used for a punch. In India the drink was probably also mixed with arrack, while on the islands of the West Indies local rum was used.

**One of sour
Two of sweet
Three of strong
Four of weak
Five drops of bitters and nutmeg spice
Serve well-chilled with lots of ice**

The sour part is mostly lime juice, sweet is sugar, and strong a local rum. For the weak part, tea was traditionally used, later a fruit juice, ginger ale or another lemonade. Many famous Tiki drinks such as the Mai Tai adhere to this ratio.

# COCKTAILS

## Ti' Punch

The Ti' Punch (from Petit Punch) is the punch variety of the French colonies. By leaving out the "weak" part, the taste of the spirit remains more distinctively in the foreground. Closely related to the Cuban daiquiri and the Brazilian caipirinha, it is no doubt the best way to drink a white rhum agricole. There are as many recipes as there are rum drinkers in the French overseas territories. Mostly, however, a couple of limes, a bottle of rhum agricole, and sugar syrup are simply put on the table. The motto that accompanies this: "chacun prepare sa propre mort" (everyone prepares their own death).

A recipe as a reference:

**1/4 cane syrup**
**3/4 of white rhum agricole**
**1 piece of lime**

# COCKTAILS

## Daiquiri

In the Cuban settlement Daiquiri, two American mining engineers are said to have mixed this for the first time in the year 1900. Because they had nothing else available apart from limes, sugar, and rum, that was what they used. This is how the story goes – even if perhaps somebody had already had the idea to mix the local rum with sugar and lime juice, it has not been verified. In all rum-producing countries, it was realized relatively quickly that these three ingredients are something like the holy trinity of the rum cocktail. This drink is actually a "sour", but its closest relatives are no doubt the caipirinha and the Ti' Punch.

However, it was a few decades later that daiquiri achieved real fame at the bar El Floridita that is in the Havana old town. Its most famous regular, Ernest Hemingway, is said to have drunk whole casks of it, which the almost equally famous barkeeper "Constante" prepared for him. As many Americans travelled to Cuba during the prohibition to indulge themselves, the cocktail soon became very widespread and popular.

A classical recipe that I learned in 2010 at a private cocktail course in Havana from a highly merited Cuban barman goes like this:

**Mix 2 bar spoons of white cane sugar and
2 cl lime juice
Add 5 cl white Cuban rum
and shake it cold on ice**

**Serve in a cocktail glass.**

# COCKTAILS

## Grog

Edward Vernon, the admiral of the Royal Navy often wore a warm cape made of grogram, a strong silk and wool fabric. This endowed him with the nickname Old Grog. As his sailors often became a bit too merry due to the state-allocated daily rum portions, he commanded in 1740 to divide the quarter of a litre per day into two rations, to dilute them with water and – against scurvy – to add a slice of lemon. This established itself throughout the British Navy and so grog was invented coincidentally. Those who had drunk a bit too much of it on shore leave and was staggering through the harbour was ridiculed with a "he's groggy". Admiral Vernon is therefore not only attributed a good drink for cold days, but also a word that is very common up until today, especially in boxing. According to recent findings, grog is supposed to have been called that even before Edward Vernon, but the story is too appealing to be totally forgotten.

**2 parts water**
**1 part Navy rum**
**lime juice to taste**
**dark cane sugar to taste**

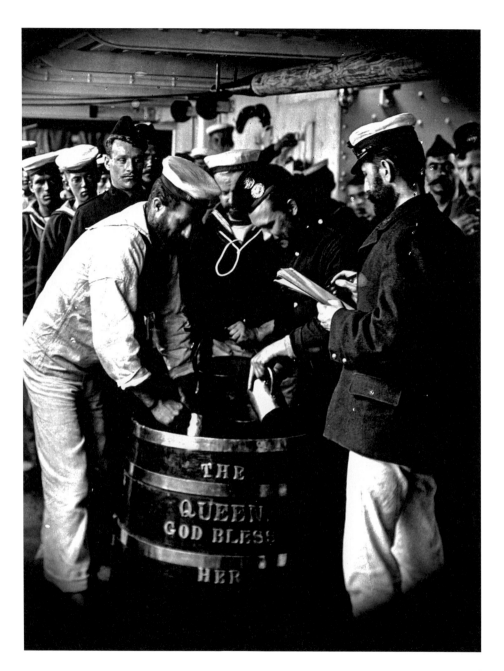

195

## SOURCES AND BIBLIOGRAPHY

**BOOKS:**
BROOM, DAVE: *Rum.* Munich: Christian Verlag, 2004.
CAMPOAMO, FERNANDO G.: *El hijo alegre de la caña de Azúcar. Biografía del ron.*
Havana: Cientifico Tecnica, 1993.
COULOMBE, CHARLES A.: *Rum. The Epic Story of the Drink That Conquered the World.*
New York: Citadel Press, 2005.
CURTIS, WAYNE.: *And a Bottle of Rum. History of the New World in Ten Cocktails.*
New York: Three Rivers Press, 2006.
GARGANO, LUCA.: *Atlas du rhum. Distilleries des Caraïbes et dégustation.*
Paris: Flammarion, 2014.
HAMILTON, EDWARD.: *Das Rum-Buch.* Munich: Lichtenberg, 1998.
LABAT, JEAN-BAPTISTE.: *Pater Labats Sklavenbericht. Abenteuerliche Jahre in der Karibik
1690–1705.* Stuttgart: Thienemann, 1984.
LIGON, RICHARD.: *A True and Exact History of the Island of Barbados.*
Indianapolis: Hackett Publishing, 2011.
PARKER, MATTHEW.: *The Sugar Barons. Family, Corruption, Empire, and War in the West Indies.*
New York: Walker Publishing, 2011.
PIERINI, MARCO.: *American Rum. A Short History of Rum in Early America.*
Createspace Independent Publishing Platform, U.S.A., 2017.
TRADER, VIC.: *Bartender's Guide.* New York: Garden City, 1948.


**ONLINE:**
www.barrel-aged-thoughts.blogspot.ch
www.ministryofrum.com
www.cocktailwonk.com
www.diffordsguide.com
www.rumportal.com
www.jamaicasugar.org/FactoryHistory/FactoryHistory.html
as well as the respective official company websites.


**PHOTOS:**
See captions. If not indicated otherwise, the photos are by Pascal Kählin.

## THE AUTHOR
Pascal Kählin, born in 1973, has been working with spirits for twenty-five years. He is the co-proprietor of two bars and a spirits shop in Zurich and is the rum attaché of the Swiss distillery Humbel. He also works as a bottler under the name "Cave Guildive".

## ACKNOWLEDGEMENTS
Werner Girsberger, Benoît Bail, Kristina Wolf, Lorenz Humbel, Oliver Schmuki

**IMPRINT**

**TEXTS**
Pascal Kählin, Sina Bühler
**GRAPHIC DESIGN**
Jonas Schwarz
**TYPESETTING**
frei – büro für gestaltung gmbh
**PICTOGRAMS**
Michael Schoch
**TRANSLATION**
Lynne Kolar-Thompson
**PROOFREADING**
Charlotte Eckler
**PRINTING AND BINDING**
DZA Druckerei zu Altenburg GmbH
**PUBLISHED BY**
Alambic Books GmbH
Brauerstrasse 51
8004 Zurich
Switzerland
www.alambic-books.com
info@alambic-books.com

© 2019 Alambic Books GmbH, Zürich

All rights reserved: no part of this work may be reproduced in any form without the prior written permission of the publishing house or processed, copied or distributed using electronic systems.

ISBN 978-3-907203-01-9

ALAMBIC
BOOKS